LECTURES ON HUMANISM

The Ethical Library

LECTURES

ON

HUMANISM

WITH SPECIAL REFERENCE TO ITS
BEARINGS ON SOCIOLOGY

BY

J. S. MACKENZIE

*M.A., Glasgow; Litt.D., Cambridge; Professor of Philosophy
in University College, Cardiff*

AUTHOR OF

"OUTLINES OF METAPHYSICS," "A MANUAL OF ETHICS"
AND "AN INTRODUCTION TO SOCIAL PHILOSOPHY"

ARDVA QVÆ PVLCRA

1709
LONDON

SWAN SONNENSCHEIN & CO., Lim.
NEW YORK: THE MACMILLAN CO.
1907

PREFATORY NOTE

IN the Lent Term, 1906, the author was called upon to undertake the duties of the Dunkin Lectureship in Sociology at Manchester College, Oxford. The courses of lectures on this foundation are short and open to the public, and hardly provide scope for the discussion of the fundamental principles of Sociology as a science. They are, consequently, concerned in general either with some special social problem or with philosophical considerations bearing, more or less directly, on social life. For the present course the subject of "Humanism" was selected, as having a special interest at that particular time and place. The object of the lectures, however, was not to discuss recent philosophical theories that have been put forward under this name, but rather to bring out the wider bearings of the point of view that seems to be more properly characterized by it.

Courses of lectures of this kind are intended to have a certain general interest; and it is, as a rule, desirable that the substance of them should be published. In the present case, however, the time for previous preparation being very limited, the lectures were delivered from rough notes; and it has not been found possible to reproduce them quite in the form in which they were originally given. It appeared, moreover, that any value that the lectures might possess would be considerably enhanced by a fuller statement of the philosophical implications of the point of view indicated in them than it had seemed possible to provide in the lectures themselves. An additional lecture has, accordingly, been inserted at the end for this purpose.

A short course such as this must necessarily appear very sketchy and inadequate. One can hardly hope that it will do more than awaken reflection, and suggest directions in which further light may be sought. But even this is probably worth doing, especially at a time when the importance of philosophical principles in the general life of mankind is becoming more and more apparent. The concluding lecture contains hints of ideas which the author hopes shortly to be able to develop more fully.

It should be mentioned that a previous course of lectures on the same foundation, by Professor Henry Jones, which was published in the *Hibbert Journal*, is written from a point of view substantially similar; but the problems with which it deals are, to a considerable extent, different.

I ought to add also that, in preparing these lectures for the press, I have received many useful suggestions from my friend, Professor Muirhead, the Editor of the series in which the book appears.

UNIVERSITY COLLEGE, CARDIFF
April, 1907

CONTENTS

LECTURES ON HUMANISM

LECTURE I

THE MEANING OF HUMANISM

THESE lectures are not directly concerned with sociology—a subject, indeed, which has not as yet assumed any definite form, and which, consequently, serves to cover many heterogeneous discussions; but they are, at least, on that general movement of thought out of which, more than anything else, such study of sociology as we have had has been developed, and by increasing contact with which I believe it must continue to grow. It has seemed to me that an attempt, however inadequate, to focus that general movement—to see whence it comes and whither it tends—may be of some value at the present time.

I have called this general movement humanistic; and, speaking in Oxford at the present time, I ought perhaps to explain at once that I do not use the term in quite that sense that has recently been given to it by a certain school of your younger writers. I do not use it as equivalent to what is more commonly—and I think more correctly—described as "pragmatism," or "voluntarism"; though I regard pragmatism as one of the special forms in which humanism has appeared—a highly typical form, and, for the moment at least, a highly interesting form, and one to which it will certainly be necessary to give some attention in what follows. But it is my object to consider the humanistic movement in a somewhat larger sense than this.

What I understand by humanism may be most simply described as a point of view from which human life is regarded as an independent centre of interest, if not even as containing within itself the key to all other interests, or as being, in old Greek phraseology, the "helm" by which the universe is steered. In this sense I contrast it with the more familiar term "naturalism"—the attempt to understand human life in the light of the forces that operate in the world around it—and also with supernaturalism, that which seeks for the explanation of the world in powers that are in their nature distinct both from man and from the world in which he lives. If a certain degree of vagueness still clings to these expressions, this is, I believe, inevitable from the nature of the subject. The antitheses which are summed up in these words depend on distinctions

that cannot in the end be maintained *—at least, in
the form in which they at first present themselves.
Yet they have played so great a part in the development of human thought and life, that they can never
altogether lose their interest and importance. There
is, on the whole, a sharp contrast between these
three ways of regarding the world and human life,
and especially between humanism and the other two.
From both the other points of view the course of
human life is apt to appear, in the phrase of Mr.
Balfour,† as " a brief and transitory episode in the
life of one of the meanest of the planets " ; whereas,
from the point of view of humanism, it is only by
reference to man's life that the rest of the universe
gains dignity and significance.

The bearing of this general standpoint upon the
study of sociology is perhaps sufficiently apparent.
It is true that many sociologists might properly be
described as naturalists. Sociology has sometimes
been treated as a department of biology, rather than
as a specifically humane study. The writings of

* This is brought out below, in Lecture VIII. The three
points of view here referred to derive their significance from the
emphasis which they lay on certain aspects of experience, which
cannot, in the end, be separated from one another. It is a large
part of my object in these lectures to bring out this insepara-
bility, by dwelling more particularly on one of the aspects, which
seems to have a special importance at the present time.

† *Foundations of Belief*, Part I, chap. i.

Herbert Spencer illustrate this tendency ; and others are even more emphatically naturalistic. Indeed, it seems clear that any serious study of sociology must carry us far beyond the limits of humanity. As a recent epitomizer * reminds us, while man is the only one of the vertebrates who has a highly developed social system, it is much lower in the scale of life that we must look for the foundations of social organization. " No mammals save man, no birds or fishes or reptiles, display any social structure that can for one moment be named beside the societies of the social ants and bees and wasps." Such considerations send us pretty far down in the scale of life ; and for anything that could be called the real beginning, it would no doubt be necessary to go still lower. Yet it is, on the whole, true that the recent developments of sociology have been prompted by a humanistic rather than by a naturalistic interest. Comte, at any rate, and those who have been chiefly affected by his influence in this country, have understood sociology very largely as an effort to substitute a more humane view of social tendencies for those somewhat mechanical conceptions of the forces that operate in human life which we find prevailing in eighteenth-century philosophy and in the older school of political economists. In

* Dr. C. W. Saleeby, *Sociology*.

opposition to these mechanical or, at any rate, mainly naturalistic theories, it has been a chief object of the sociologists to urge that man's life must be treated somewhat differently from the forces of nature, and this on the twofold ground that we cannot properly forget, in dealing with human affairs, that man has a history, which modifies the conditions of his life, and that he has a more or less conscious end.

That man has a history is, in particular, the point that has been persistently emphasized by our sociologists and sociological economists.* In a sense, of course, it is the great lesson of our modern age that the whole world, animate and inanimate, has a history behind it that must be carefully studied if we are ever rightly to understand it. But man is the only being in the world who carries his history along with him. His history not merely behind him, but is a constantly living force in his present. He has history, as well as *a* history—a record and a forecast, as well as a growing life. This, I take it, is the most fundamental point in the doctrine of the historical school in economics ; and it is chiefly by that school that the importance of sociological studies has been emphasized. The growth of sociology may thus be

* e.g. Cliffe Leslie, Ingram, etc.

regarded as an aspect of the more general growth
of interest in human history.

So long, however, as it is only this historical
aspect that is brought forward, the distinctively
humanistic aspect of sociological studies is not
fully apparent. Though history belongs emphatically to man, it does not belong to him exclusively ;
and a study is not absolutely stamped as humanistic
by the fact that it is historical. The fact that
it involves a reference to conscious ends is more
definitely characteristic. Now, it cannot be said
that this point has always been prominently set
forth in sociological studies, or even that it has
always been recognized at all by those whose names
are chiefly associated with such studies. The emphasis on ends is to be found rather in the ethical
than in the historical school of economic and social
studies. It is connected with the names of Carlyle
and Ruskin rather than with those of Comte, Cliffe
Leslie, or Ingram ; and the names of Carlyle and
Ruskin are not usually associated with the study of
sociology, in the sense in which that term is most
commonly understood. The essential point in the
teaching of Ruskin, in particular, is his insistence
that the instruments and external conditions of
human development must be considered in constant
relation to the ultimate end that is subserved by

them ; in other words, that the point of view in the study of human affairs must be teleological. This is what is expressed in his declaration that " the only Wealth is Life " ; and also in the view which he takes of fine art, as not existing for its own sake, but for the expression of noble thoughts about life.

This teleological view of the facts of human life, however, does in reality connect very closely with the other point to which I have referred—viz. that man has a history. For, though the term " history is sometimes used in such a way as simply to imply a record of events or series of changes, it usually carries with it some further implications. Human history is, more and more, seen to be a record of the gradual working out of certain tendencies ; and these tendencies can hardly be properly understood without reference to the ends to which they point. It is doubtful, of course, whether even the natural history of animal life can be properly understood without some teleological interpretation. Even if it is maintained that animal life is to be interpreted as a mere struggle for existence, still the effort to maintain existence implies, at least, an unconscious end. But when we say that human life involves history in a more complete sense than that in which it can be ascribed to animal life, the meaning is partly that the ends that are struggled for have come out into clearer consciousness. The development of animal life presents, relatively, a haphazard appearance. Types happen to be evolved ; and some of them happen to survive. Human life is, in Mr. Hobhouse's phrase,* much more definitely " orthogenic " ; it is a progress towards a goal more or less definitely regarded as good. In this sense, therefore, the fact that man has a history is only another aspect of the fact that he has a conscious end.

Indeed, both these points rest on the still more fundamental fact that man has a mind—that he is " a being of a large discourse, looking before and after." His past and his future have a present significance for him, such as we are not entitled to assume in the case of any other being that we know. The past and the future have indeed a certain significance for all animal beings. The present tendencies of an animal are the outcome of the past experience of its species ; and they point to ends which are to be realized in its future life, or in that of its species. Its past and its future have a meaning ; but it does not know what that meaning is.†

* *Mind in Evolution*, p. 5. The term " aristogenic " had been previously used by Mr. Sutherland (*Origin and Growth of the Moral Instinct*, Vol. I, p. 29).

† The nature of animal consciousness is of course a somewhat controversial point ; and I do not wish to dogmatize upon it here. The view that I take of it, and that justifies the antithesis above suggested, is derived, in the main, from such works as Lloyd Morgan's *Animal Life and Intelligence* and Stout's *Manual of Psychology*.

The essential difference, in the case of human life, is that man does, with more or less clearness, apprehend the significance both of his past and of his future, and that his actions are largely guided by this apprehension. It is this circumstance that makes it really impossible to treat sociology as a branch of biology; and it is this aspect of sociological study that I aim at bringing out in the present course of lectures.

Looking at the matter in this way, what we have to consider is not merely the historical treatment of human life, nor even the ethical conception of it as directed to the realization of the highest good, but rather the more general conception of the way in which the life of a thinking being has to be regarded; and, indeed, it is only on this ground that I, as a student of philosophy, whose main interest lies in metaphysics and ethics, have any justification in dealing with the subject at all. From this point of view, the work of the German idealists and their English followers—especially the attempts made by these to construct a philosophy of history and a philosophical theory of the state—have quite as much relevance as the writings of the historical economists and sociologists, or of such social moralists as Carlyle and Ruskin.

These remarks may perhaps enable you to see, in

a general way, what I understand by humanism, and how it bears upon the study of sociology. It means a point of view contrasted with naturalism ; and, in special relation to sociology, it means a method of studying the facts of social life based on the recognition that human life cannot be dealt with quite as the facts of unthinking nature may. It is opposed, for instance, as I have already indicated, to the somewhat mechanical conceptions that are connected with some of the older (and, indeed, also with some of the newer) writings on political economy. It may be contrasted also with such a dictum as that of Spinoza, that we should study human life just as if we were studying a circle or triangle.* And, though it is quite true that this contrast is by no means always apparent in the works of sociologists, yet it may, at least, be fairly maintained that it is distinctly traceable in the attitude of Comte himself, who, more than any other in modern times, has claims to be regarded as the founder of the science. From the point of view of Comte, man's life occupies a unique position. Humanity is for him a great being, which may fit-

* What Spinoza has chiefly in view is of course the importance of studying human life with the same dispassionateness as that with which we usually study geometry ; but the statement tends with him to imply also the same absence of teleological reference (see Lecture II).

tingly be taken as an object of worship, and which is struggling towards an end intrinsically higher than any that can be discovered in the world around him. It seems clear that it was this conception of humanity that served as the inspiring force in leading Comte to lay the foundations of the science of sociology.

Now, it is not my intention here to lecture directly upon Comte, or even to lecture directly upon sociology ; but, if I may so put it, I intend to lecture round these subjects, which, I hope, need not mean that the lectures will be rambling and disconnected, though, of course, it does mean that they will not be, in any full sense, systematic. It is evident that the humanistic movement, as I here conceive it, has a much larger significance than could be discovered by simply directing our attention to Comte ; and its results go far beyond the limits of the study of sociology, even on the widest interpretation of that somewhat elastic term ; and, though I wish to keep its sociological bearings constantly in mind, it is also my aim to open up some of its larger aspects.

There is, however, one point in the teaching of Comte which may serve as a convenient starting-point—I mean his doctrine of the " three stages " in the development of human thought. You are no doubt aware that Comte represented human thought as passing through three successive phases, which he expressed by the terms "theological," "meta-physical," and "positive." The meaning is that men tend at first to interpret the occurrences in the world around them by ascribing them to the action of divine personalities ; that they afterwards modify this by ascribing them to occult forces not conceived as personal ; and that they learn, finally, to be content with giving a positive account of what takes place, without attempting any ultimate explanation. It seems clear that there is some justification for this account of the tendencies of human thought ; and it would carry me rather too far away from the scope of my subject if I were to attempt to criticize it. I must content myself with stating that it seems to me somewhat incomplete and arbitrary, and that I believe we should arrive at a more adequate view of the development of human thought if we were to substitute for Comte's three terms the closely related terms "supernaturalism," "naturalism," and "humanism." At least, I would claim that this may serve as a convenient variant upon Comte's arrangement, and may help to make my general meaning in these lectures clear. The first of the terms that I here employ would practically cover the first two of Comte's "stages." Whether we explain things by divine personalities or by occult non-personal forces, the explanation may in either

case be said to be supernatural. It accounts for
the course of things by something outside that
course, and conceived as in some way superior in
potency. Whether it is regarded as personal or
as impersonal, is a somewhat subordinate point,
and I am not sure that it can be fairly held that the
former mode of conceiving it tends uniformly to be
prior to the latter. Both, at any rate, are covered
by the term "supernaturalism." Naturalism, on
the other hand, corresponds pretty closely to what
Comte calls positivism.* It is the attempt to
interpret the world around us in its own light, without reference to any extraneous beings or powers.
This description, however, does not quite suffice to
distinguish it from what I here understand by
humanism, which also refrains from any appeal
to occult or extraneous powers. The difference is
that, while naturalism bases its interpretation of
the world on objects as they are presented to us,
humanism points us rather to the thinking subject
for the interpretation of all that comes before it.

* It tends at least, more and more, to pass into positivism,
though at first it takes a form which might almost be described
as metaphysical in Comte's sense—e.g. the form represented by
the Cartesians and even by Hobbes, as contrasted with that
represented by Hume and, in general, by the modern natural
sciences. For some remarks bearing on the relations between
positivism and naturalism, I may refer to Mill's *Auguste Comte
and Positivism*, Part I, and to Mr. Balfour's *Foundations of
Belief*, Part I, chap. i.

This may perhaps serve to indicate what I understand by humanism, and how I conceive it to be related to other points of view. Humanism, as I here understand it, may be described in general as the attitude of mind which seeks the key to the world in the life of man, or, at any rate, the key to man's life within himself.

Having given this general indication of what I understand by humanism, I may now explain briefly the line that I intend to pursue in dealing with it in these lectures. First, I must try to make the exact meaning of the humanistic position a little clearer, and to show more definitely its significance in human thought. Then I intend to illustrate the development of this point of view by reference to the general history of philosophy, both in ancient and in modern times. After this, it will be possible to bring out more definitely the philosophical implications of the ideas that underlie it. Then we shall be able to consider the application of these ideas in some of the leading aspects of life ; and it is here, of course, that we shall be touching most definitely upon the subject of sociology. Finally I intend to attempt a brief critical estimate of the humanistic position, bringing out certain limitations that are apt to be involved in it, and indicating what I conceive to be the more excellent way.

I have said that humanism is to be understood as meaning the view that we are to seek for the key to the universe in man, or, at any rate, for the key to man's life within himself. Evidently there is a good deal of difference between these two things ; and, though the difference may not appear at first to affect very materially those more purely practical aspects of the subject, with which we are here mainly concerned, yet it does really affect even these, and it is, consequently, of some importance that we should take note of this difference at the outset. There are, indeed, a considerable number of different shades of meaning with which the term may be intelligibly used ; but it will probably suffice to distinguish three. (1) It might mean that man's life is to be studied and interpreted in a certain way which is peculiar to itself, and that the rest of the universe may, for this purpose, be entirely or largely left out of account. This may, I think, be fairly said to have been the point of view of Socrates ; and, somewhat less definitely, it is no doubt what is in the minds of most of those who urge that " the proper study of mankind is man." If we confine ourselves to this, however, the doctrine has not much philosophical significance, nor can it very well defend itself against any theory that seeks to explain man's life in relation to the rest of the universe.

(2) It might mean that we find in man's life the complete key to the life of the universe—that, in the end, whatever presents itself as foreign to man's life must be regarded as non-existent, illusory, or negligible. This view, however, also assumes several different forms. In particular, it may be interpreted in a more sceptical and in a more constructive fashion. The more sceptical sense is that which is specially associated with the name of Protagoras, and with his famous *dictum* that "man is the measure of all things." He seems to have meant by this that it is not really possible to get beyond the human point of view, and that it is consequently our wisest plan, like Voltaire's Candide, to "cultivate our gardens," and not trouble about realities beyond our reach.* Even this view, however, may be interpreted in different ways, according as we think of the human point of view as being one that is valid for us all, or as one that varies with different individuals, or as one that is partly variable and partly constant. In contrast with such more or less sceptical attitudes, there is the positive doctrine

* Thus understood, humanism would scarcely be distinguishable from naturalism or positivism, except by its more decidedly sceptical character. "Philosophic doubt," as understood by Mr. Balfour, seems to approximate at least to the type of humanism here described. So also does "pragmatism" in some of the forms in which it is put forward, especially by Mr. Schiller.

—best represented perhaps by Bishop Berkeley—
that the human mind, and other minds like man's,
are the only things that really exist, and consequently that in studying man we are truly studying
everything. It is clear that these various positions
are widely different, though, for our present purpose,
they may be summed up under a single heading.
(3) It might mean that man's life furnishes us with
a key which opens up to us the secrets of the universe
more adequately than any other that can be used, but
that it must, nevertheless, be constantly considered
in relation to the other aspects of our experience.
This I take to be the view of Plato, and, in general,
of those who are described as idealists in philosophy
—when that term is not used, as it very commonly
is, to characterize such a position as that of Berkeley.*

These various views tend to glide almost imper-
ceptibly into one another, so that it is hardly possible
to keep them apart. It is evident also that it would
carry us far beyond the scope of such a course of
lectures as this if we were to attempt to discuss all
these different positions and their relations to one
another. What we have here in hand is a much
more modest undertaking. My chief object is to
bring before your minds the fact that there is a

* These points are somewhat more fully considered in
Lectures VIII and IX.

C

point of view that may be described as emphatically humanistic, a point of view that concentrates attention on the study of human life, and that seeks to distinguish itself from the point of view of naturalism according to which man's life is only a part, and a comparatively insignificant part, of the system of nature. I do not think that we can proceed very far with the consideration of this point of view without opening up some of the most difficult problems of metaphysics. The attempt of Socrates to study the life of man, apart from the system of the universe, led very speedily to the speculative constructions of Plato and Aristotle, and I am inclined to think that some such transition must inevitably take place. Yet it may be profitable to consider what is meant by a humanistic standpoint, with reference to some of the leading problems of life, even if we must largely set aside the discussion of the ultimate implications of such a standpoint. It seems to me, however, that, even with this somewhat limited object in view, it is necessary to begin with the consideration of some points relating to general philosophy. I now proceed, accordingly, to give some illustrations of the way in which what I describe as a humanistic standpoint has come out in the development of philosophic thought.

The finest historical illustration of the spirit of

humanism, in the broad sense in which I am here understanding it, is certainly to be found, not in connection with the teaching of Comte or that of the recent Pragmatists, or with any other form of modern thought, but rather in the most flourishing period of Greek speculation—the period in which the real foundations of sociology, as of almost every other scientific study, were first laid. The Greeks, indeed, strike one on the whole as born humanists. They played the game of life, as Goethe said, more beautifully than any others, and their centre of interest seemed always to lie in life. They were not called upon by the conditions of their lives, like most modern peoples, to put forth great efforts for the subjugation of natural forces ; they did not get captured by an imperial mission, like that of the Romans ; nor was it their tendency, like most Oriental peoples, to seek peace in the contemplation of the absolute and infinite. To be men, and to play the game of life beautifully, seemed rather to be their highest ambition. Their religion, their art, their literature, were all eminently humane ; and it was but natural that in the end their scientific speculations should have the same characteristics. Yet at first the tendency of Greek thought, like that of other peoples, was towards supernaturalism — and, indeed, towards a form of supernaturalism that leant more to naturalism than to humanism. Perhaps I cannot better bring out what I mean by the distinctions between these attitudes of mind than by directing your attention to the way in which Greek thought developed.

The earliest attempts of the Greeks to give an account of the world in which they found themselves—such as those of Hesiod and Homer—are undoubtedly steeped in supernaturalism. Everything is accounted for by the action of gods ; and, though these gods are represented in human form, their kinship is evidently in the main with the forces of nature, rather than with the activities of the human mind. As soon as clear thought began among the Greeks, however, we find this supernaturalism rapidly giving place to an almost pure Naturalism. In Xenophanes the popular theory is turned into ridicule, and the "guesses something like the truth," which he seeks to substitute for it, have a highly naturalistic air ; and this is, on the whole, carried out consistently throughout the development of early Greek thought.

The materialism of the early Greek philosophers, from Thales to Democritus, has tended no doubt to be a good deal exaggerated. They were essentially hylozoists, and a certain element of what may almost be characterized as humanism underlay even their most materialistic speculations. When, for instance, they emphasized air as one of the most fundamental of the elements, they were thinking very largely of the breath of life ; and, though Anaxagoras seemed to Aristotle a sober man among idle babblers, on account of his introduction of mind as a principle of interpretation, mind was not really far from the thoughts of any of them. Still, it is true that these early philosophers, including Anaxagoras himself, looked only, as Aristotle put it, for a material explanation. Looking at the world around them, they sought simply to analyse it into its elements ; and thus they may, fairly enough, be characterized as early naturalists, or even positivists.*

The great movement, on the other hand, represented by the sophists and Socrates, was in the main humanistic. It was a return to the life of man

---

* By far the most interesting account of these primitive thinkers is that contained in Burnet's *Early Greek Philosophy* ; but I think Professor Burnet exaggerates very considerably the materialistic tendency of their thought. What seems to be true of all of them is that they have not learned to distinguish between the material world and the world of conscious life ; and that their theories of the universe tend to be expressed almost entirely in terms of the former. This is as true, on the whole, of Parmenides and Anaxagoras—the real founders of the Athenian school of idealism—as it is of any of the others. But that any of them meant to set forth a materialistic theory of the universe, in the sense in which a modern writer might do so, seems clearly untrue.

from the more or less futile effort to interpret the outside world. No doubt it might be said, in the language of Comte, to have gone primarily in the direction of positivism. It was an abandonment, not only of supernatural personalities, but also of those metaphysical entities upon which the earlier philosophers had relied for their interpretations. But this positivism was, at any rate, accompanied by a fresh interest in human life, and a fresh tendency to look in human life for the key to the world around. We see the most distinct evidence of this in the teaching of Protagoras. That " man is the measure of all things " meant partly with him, as with the modern pragmatists, the despair of any ultimate objective criterion. But there can be little doubt that it meant also, as with the pragmatists, a certain satisfaction with the purely human standpoint—a conviction that, from this standpoint, some really valuable insight can be attained.

It is with Socrates, however, that we most definitely pass over from naturalism to humanism. Socrates appears, more definitely than any of the sophists, to have renounced the attempt to interpret the natural world. But this definite renunciation was accompanied by the strenuous endeavour to understand the inner nature of man himself. Like our modern pragmatists, he tended to interpret man's life mainly with reference to his endeavours to achieve certain practical results. He thought of life as an art, aiming at a definite end, like the art of sculpture or shoe-making, and he conceived that it could be fully understood by means of the clear definition of the object at which it aims. As against the scepticism that tended to prevail among the sophists, he held that there is a real science of human nature, but that it is a science of a very different character from any of the natural sciences. It is a science whose content lies ready to hand within ourselves, requiring only to be brought out by reflection and discussion. The content, moreover, consists in the main, not of facts, but of purposes. If man is the measure or standard of all things, the standard is at least a being with principles and purposes capable of being exactly understood and estimated. If there can be no objective science of anything else, there can at any rate be an objective science of man himself, as a being with an end, which is capable of being brought into clear self-consciousness by reflection. It is thus that Socrates substitutes a humanistic position for the previous naturalism or positivism.*

* The articles on the Sophists and on Socrates by Dr. H. Jackson in the ninth edition of the *Encyclopædia Britannica* will be found very instructive from the point of view here indicated.

The humanism of Socrates, however, meant that man is to be treated as a thing apart. The rest of the world is left over for naturalism or for scepticism.* Hence Socrates can hardly be called a humanist in the full sense in which I have sought to use the term. Man is man, he urges, a being with an end, with a clearly definable purpose, not resolvable into water or fire, or even into the vaguer νοῦς. But the world may otherwise be interpreted as we will, or left without any interpretation. But, once it has been insisted that one being can be satisfactorily interpreted on a certain basis, it is hardly possible to rest there. If one being is fully intelligible, the world in which he lives, and of which he is a part, can hardly be an entirely unintelligible world. Nor, indeed, can it very well be supposed to be a world that is to be understood on some entirely different principle. And thus the point of view of Socrates almost inevitably presses us forward to that of Plato and Aristotle.†

Plato, as we know, connected the point of view of Socrates with that of Anaxagoras. If we are to

---

* It would seem, however, from a passage in Xenophon's *Memorabilia*, that Socrates did suggest the application of the idea of end to nature as well as to man (cf. Caird's *Development of Theology in Greek Philosophy*, Lecture III).

† The significance of this is more fully brought out in Lectures VIII and IX.

interpret man's life in the light of purpose, we are almost inevitably driven to interpret the life of the universe in the same way ; and this is very naturally taken to be the meaning of the doctrine of Anaxagoras, that *νοῦς* puts all things in order. The interpretation of the world then ceases to be thought of as possible through the analysis of the elements of which it is composed ; and is regarded rather as taking place through an indication of its meaning, or of that at which it aims. This of course is the point of view that is developed in Plato's theory of ideas or types—a doctrine which must be regarded as being, in its essence, though not always in its details, humanistic. It is an attempt to interpret the universe in the same way in which we naturally interpret our own thoughts and aspirations.*

The doctrine of Aristotle differs from that of Socrates and Plato chiefly through the introduction of the idea of history or process. The end for

---

* The chief qualification to this is to be found in the Pythagorean element in the Platonic system—the tendency to interpret the ideas as geometrical or arithmetical forms. It is chiefly this that prevents Plato from being, in any full sense, humanistic. Another important qualification is seen in the more mystical and mythological aspects of his teaching, which often give to his philosophy a certain appearance of supernaturalism. This side of his teaching has been specially emphasized in recent times by Professor Stewart (*The Myths of Plato*). But, indeed, as I indicated at the outset, these antitheses cannot, in the end, be maintained (cf. Lectures VII, VIII, and IX).

Socrates seems to be merely something that he finds
within his own consciousness.   For Plato it is the
secret of the universe, but a secret laid up, as it were,
apart—a treasure in heaven, which is only de-
graded by its presentation upon earth.   For Aristotle it is implicit in the life of the world.   The
world is thus conceived as unfolding its meaning,
somewhat as a man works out his purpose.   This
is what I understand by humanism, in its fullest
sense.   It is the point of view that marks the cul-
mination of Greek speculative thought, and, in the
systems that followed in the period of its decline,*
this standpoint was never wholly lost.

This brief outline of the course of development
of Greek speculative thought may enable you to see
the exact sense in which I am here seeking to understand the term humanism.   My point is that, in
trying to understand the world in which we are and
our own lives in it, we at a very early stage become
aware of the striking antithesis between the natural
world, with its various forms of matter and motion,
and the human world, with its purposes and ideals ;
and that we are forced either to try to explain the
one in terms of the other, or to seek for different

* Its decline as *pure speculation*.   From some other points of
view, it is possible to regard these later developments as an
advance.   This is very finely brought in in Caird's *Development
of Theology in Greek Philosophy.*

methods of explanation in the two cases, or to explain both by something that goes beyond them, or to admit that any ultimately satisfactory explanations are impossible. Naturalism I take to be, in general terms, the attempt to understand the world by reference to matter and motion and other cognate conceptions. Humanism, on the other hand, is, in similarly general terms, the attempt to understand the world by reference to thought and purpose and other cognate conceptions. The nature of this antithesis, however, may, I think, be brought out still more distinctly by a brief reference to the development of modern views of the world.

Indeed, the term humanism is most commonly used to designate a movement at the beginning of the modern age, in which the influence of Greek thought was to a considerable extent revived. It was mainly a movement of revolt against medieval ecclesiasticism ; and its general outcome is summed up for us in the couplet of Pope :—

> " Know then thyself ; presume not God to scan ;
> The proper study of mankind is man."

But this transient glimpse of the humanistic spirit was swallowed up again, very speedily, in a new naturalism ; and it is only in comparatively recent times that a genuine modern humanism can be said to have come to birth. Comte, as I have already indicated, may be taken as one of the chief representatives of such a movement ; but we may at least fairly say that he was preceded by Rousseau, and that the great movement of German idealism, growing out of Leibniz, and proceeding onwards through Kant and his successors, represents a still more striking development in a similar direction. The study of these more modern lines of advance, however—even in the very sketchy fashion that is alone possible in such a course as this—seems to demand a separate lecture.

LECTURE II

THE GROWTH OF HUMANISM

THE humanism which grew out of the Renaissance—which, indeed, we might almost say, was the inner meaning of the Renaissance—was certainly not, in any special way, opposed to naturalism, but rather to ecclesiasticism and tradition. It was, indeed, almost as much a naturalism as a humanism. It was a return to man and nature from the trammels of an artificial system of life and thought, based upon a supernatural conception of the world. It was in opposition to this cramping view that men turned to the freedom of an earlier age, and especially caught inspiration from the poetry, art, and philosophy of Greece, and even from the feebler reflection of these among the Romans. And it was of course essentially the same naturalistic and humanistic spirit that led up gradually to the great religious reformation, under the influence of which we still live.

Luther and Bacon have been, not altogether

fancifully, compared * as having both emphasized
the supreme duty of private judgment, the one in
religion, the other in science. They both appealed
to a direct human experience as the only secure
basis for real insight. On the more purely philosophical side, a similar attitude of mind is seen in
Descartes. The first principle of his philosophy—
—his *cogito ergo sum*—expresses the conviction that
it is only what appeals to us with the direct evidence
of personal experience that can be regarded as
certain knowledge. Living personal contact with
facts may thus be said to be what is mainly emphasized, alike by Luther, by Bacon, and by Descartes. They all rest on the experience of man ;
and, in this way at least, their point of view may
be compared with that of Protogoras, or with that
of Socrates, in the ancient world ; and it may, in a
broad sense, be characterized as humanistic.

This kind of humanism, however, as I have already indicated, passes very easily into naturalism ;
and on the whole it was in this direction that it
tended to move. Bacon, for instance, has no
doubt some of the makings of a humanist, and is
closely connected with the great humanists of the
Elizabethan age ; but in the main he is a naturalist.
His great aim is to make the human mind into a

* E. Caird, *Critical Philosophy of Kant*, Vol. I, p. 72.

clear mirror of nature. He is an avowed foe of Plato and Aristotle, and commends rather the work of Leucippus and Democritus, thinking that the stream of time, like a river, has carried down the lighter materials, and let the weightier and more solid drop. The same tendency is seen in Hobbes. Spinoza, again, leads us to *deus sive natura*, rather than to *homo* ; * and one wonders in the end how the simple *cogito* of Descartes could ever have led him so far away from the direct experience of mankind. And, indeed, the whole of the succeeding age is characterized by the steady development of the mathematical and physical sciences, much more than by any deepening insight into the facts and experiences of human life. Even when men, like Hobbes himself, or like Locke and others in later times, turned their attention largely to psychology and ethics, they tended to carry with them to these studies the methods and habits of thought that are naturally formed in the investigation of the material world.

Cartesianism, in particular, may be taken as representing, in its ultimate development and under-

---

* In the case of Spinoza, however, this is certainly subject to very large qualifications. It would perhaps be truest to say that he is a humanist who habitually expresses himself in the language either of naturalism or of supernaturalism—at least in his more strictly philosophical writings.

lying tendencies, one of the most characteristic phases of modern naturalism ; just as the pre-Socratic philosophers represent that of the ancient world. Indeed, these two lines of development have much in common. A striking characteristic of both is the elimination of final causes in the explanation of the world, and the tendency to reduce all differences in the end to differences of quantity.* Of course, in the case of ancient thought, the elimination of final causes really meant that these had not yet been thought of as possible means of explanation. Even human action was hardly thought of as definitely purposive, till Socrates taught men to inquire into the nature of the end ; still less was any purpose thought of as being embodied in nature.† The elimination of quality was also, no doubt, to a large extent unconscious in early Greek thought ; and it was only by slow degrees that it was carried out with any thoroughness by the Eleatics, the Pythagoreans, and the atomists. With the modern Cartesians, on the other hand, the rejection of qualitative

* It is particularly instructive to compare Cartesianism with Pythagoreanism, on the one hand, and with Eleaticism, on the other. Like the former, it tends to interpret everything in terms of mathematical determinations ; like the latter, it tends to resolve all reality into an undifferentiated unity.

† It seems clear that this is substantially true even in the case of Anaxagoras (cf. Burnet's *Early Greek Philosophy*).

differences and final causes is conscious and systematic ; and it is this fact that gives to their philosophy, in spite of some tendencies in another direction, its highly naturalistic air.

The rejection of final causes was no doubt made at first by Descartes in a way that seems innocent enough, and not to lead to any far-reaching consequences. It appears at first simply in the form of a modest avowal that we cannot hope fully to understand the purposes for which things, as we find them, have been devised.* It is not denied, but rather assumed, that, from a more complete point of view—from the point of view of the divine consciousness—the world would be seen to be purposive throughout. This is, indeed, explicitly involved in the Cartesian conception of divine perfection. The rejection of final causes was, however, in reality based upon much deeper grounds than those that were at first avowed. It really depended on the

* Meditation IV (Veitch's translation). " Knowing already that my nature is extremely weak and limited, and that the nature of God, on the other hand, is immense, incomprehensible, and infinite, I have no longer any difficulty in discerning that there is an infinity of things in His power whose causes transcend the grasp of my mind ; and this consideration alone is sufficient to convince me, that the whole class of final causes is of no avail in physical or natural things ; for it appears to me that I cannot, without exposing myself to the charge of temerity, seek to discover the impenetrable ends of Deity."

D

general conception of scientific explanation which was involved in the Cartesian system—a conception based primarily upon the methods of mathematics. If it was true of the early Greek philosophers, as Aristotle put it, that they recognized only the material cause, it would be almost equally true to say of the Cartesians, that they recognized only the formal cause. But in reality this had been gradually coming to be true of the early Greek philosophers as well ; so that in the end there is not very much difference between them. At any rate, it is true of the Cartesians that their conception of the world tends more and more to be a formal or mathematical one ; and that it is mainly on this account that final causes are eliminated. This aspect of their philosophy, like so many others, is made fully explicit by Spinoza, who definitely points out that the Cartesian conception of divine perfection is not really compatible with any external purpose.* It is only compatible with the ex-

* Ethics, Part I, Appendix (Elwes's translation). "There is no need to show at length that nature has no particular goal in view, and that final causes are mere human figments. This is, I think, evident enough, both from the causes and foundations on which I have shown such prejudice to be based, and also from . . . all those propositions in which I have shown that everything in nature proceeds from a sort of necessity, and with the utmost perfection. However, I will add a few remarks, in order to overthrow this doctrine of a final cause utterly. That which is really a cause it considers as an effect, and vice versa ; it makes that

planation of the particular nature of the world as following from the divine nature, just as—to use Spinoza's favourite comparison—the fact of its three angles being equal to two right angles follows from the nature of a triangle.

The reduction of all differences to differences of quantity follows directly from the same general point of view. Here, again, the full significance of the position does not at first appear. It is veiled, in particular, in its first presentation by Descartes, by the fact that he retains and emphasizes the one great qualitative distinction between mind and matter. This distinction is, indeed, made so

which is by nature first to be last, and that which is highest and most perfect to be most imperfect. . . . It is plain . . . that that effect is most perfect which is produced immediately by God ; the effect which requires for its production several intermediate causes is, in that respect, more imperfect. But if those things which were made immediately by God were made to enable him to attain his end, then the things which come after, for the sake of which the first were made, are necessarily the most excellent of all.

Further, this doctrine does away with the perfection of God ; for, if God acts for an object, he necessarily desires something which He lacks. Certainly, theologians and metaphysicians draw a distinction between the object of want and the object of assimilation ; still they confess that God made all things for the sake of Himself, not for the sake of creation. They are unable to point to anything prior to creation, except God Himself, as an object for which God should act, and are therefore driven to admit (as they clearly must) that God lacked those things for whose attainment He created means, and, further, that He desired them."

absolute that one hardly notices at first that it is really being so used as to obliterate all other differences.* It does no doubt also appear at first as if another great qualitative difference were being retained—that, namely, between the finite and the infinite ; but this is soon seen to be illusory. The finite has, in the end, to be treated as absolutely unreal, except when it is regarded simply as a part of the infinite.†

In the further development of the Cartesian system,

* Qualitative differences come, more and more, to be treated by Descartes as arising from the *composite* nature of man ; and, as this composite nature is soon seen to be inconsistent with his fundamental dualism, there is hardly any place left for such differences among his followers.

† Pope's well-known summing up of the Spinozistic point of view is, in general, fair enough.

" All are but parts of one stupendous whole,
  Whose body nature is, and God the soul ;
  That, changed through all, and yet in all the same,
  Great in the earth as in the ethereal frame ;
  Warms in the sun, refreshes in the breeze,
  Glows in the stars and blossoms in the trees ;
  Lives through all life, extends through all extent,
  Spreads undivided, operates unspent ;
  Breathes in our soul, informs our mortal part,
  As full, as perfect, in a hair as heart ;
  As full, as perfect, in vile man that mourns,
  As the rapt seraph that adores and burns ;
  To him no high, no low, no great, no small ;
  He fills, he bounds, he connects, and equals all."

Of course some of the finer points in the Spinozistic system are not quite definitely represented here—especially the intrinsic identity of the two ultimate attributes, which Pope charac-

it soon appears that at least one great result of separating off the finite from the infinite and matter from mind, is to remove all qualitative differences from the world of nature. All qualitative differences in experience tend to be referred to mind, or to the interaction between mind and matter. In mind we seem to discover at least one qualitative element ; since it has a certain freedom of choice, capable of going beyond the grasp of the understanding, and giving to it a certain individuality of its own. This, of course, like so much else, disappears in Spinoza, by whom it is definitely affirmed that the will is no wider than the understanding. But

---

terizes by the terms " soul " and " body." It may be noted also that in this summing up, quantitative differences seem to disappear, as well as qualitative ; as they do also in Emerson's somewhat similar summing up—

> " There is no great and no small
> To the soul that seeth all ;
> And, where it cometh, all things are ;
> And it cometh everywhere."

But the Cartesian philosophy never quite abandons quantitative differences. At least its leading points always tend to be stated in geometrical language ; though it is no doubt true that what Spinoza ultimately means by the infinite is not intended to have a definitely quantitative significance. I think it may fairly be added that Spinoza never really succeeds in giving to the infinite any clearly intelligible meaning that is not really quantitative. He is, however, constantly endeavouring to grasp the later conception that was developed by Hegel. But this can only be made finally intelligible by the restoration of qualitative differences.

even with the other Cartesians the arbitrariness of man seems to be chiefly emphasized with the view of establishing the constancy of God and the inviolability of nature.

In nature, at any rate, we are, according to the Cartesians, in the reign of pure quantity. Here, in truth, as with the Pythagoreans, "all is number." The material world is emptied of all qualities but those that are purely spatial. Its changes are all interpreted in terms of locomotion ; and the important doctrine of the absolute conservation of the amount of motion in the universe—a partial anticipation of the more modern doctrine of the conservation of energy—is introduced. The full significance of this is once more slightly veiled— *more Cartesiano*—by its being represented, not as following from a purely mechanical theory of the universe, but as a consequence of the divine perfection and immutability.

Mind, in the meantime, seems no doubt, as I have indicated, to stand apart from the realm of nature, and to preserve its distinctive modes. It has a more or less arbitrary power of choice, especially the power of choosing wrong and falling into error and sin.* But the development of the Cartesian

* With Descartes himself, this is left very vague ; but it comes out more explicitly in Malebranche.

philosophy tended, more and more, to assimilate the world of mind to the world of matter—an assimilation which, once more, finds its logical outcome in the work of Spinoza. With Spinoza mind and matter are only two aspects of the same reality ; and the one is consequently regarded as completely parallel to the other. This tends to mean, in effect, that mind is treated on a purely naturalistic basis ; though there remain one or two points in which the parallelism of mind to matter seems difficult to work out, and in particular there remains a somewhat unaccountable vagary of the " imagination," almost comparable to the wilfulness of the Epicurean atoms, and, in reality, forming the basis for the later monadology of Leibniz.*

* In a brief sketch such as this it is of course necessary to state the leading points broadly, and without much qualification. I am well aware that there are two lines of thought in the writings of Spinoza. His primary interest (as we see from the *De intellectus emendatione*) is ethical, and consequently humanistic; and this side never entirely disappears throughout his work. Its significance has recently been very admirably brought out by Mr. R. A. Duff, in his book on Spinoza's *Political and Ethical Philosophy*. On the other hand, the more purely intellectual side of Spinoza's work is directed towards the perfecting of the mathematical system of Descartes ; and, in doing this, he is inevitably led in the direction that has been indicated above. Contrast, for instance, the following statements : " I confess I cannot understand how spirits express God more than the other creatures, for I know that between the finite and the infinite there is no proportion, and that the distinction between God and the most excellent of created things differs not a whit from

With Leibniz, it must be admitted, the general nature of this whole line of thought is greatly changed. He fixes upon and develops those elements in the Cartesian philosophy that were most difficult to reconcile with naturalism—the reality of the individual self, freedom of choice, innate potentialities, and the like—and uses them in such a way as to transform the Cartesian conception of the world, yet in a way that was at least very largely implicit in the work of Spinoza. The system of nature, regarded as a world in space, is no longer regarded as ultimately real; and final causes are reintroduced as the only mode of explanation that in the end is valid. Yet it can hardly be said that the point of view even of Leibniz is com-

the distinction between Him and the lowest and meanest of them" (Letter LVIII). " Though it is not necessary to know Christ after the flesh, it is necessary to know the eternal Son of God ; i.e. God's eternal wisdom, which is manifested in all things, but chiefly in the mind of man " (Letter XXI). It has to be recognized that Spinoza to a very large extent anticipates the humanism of the later German idealists, just as Berkeley does, but in an even more remarkable degree. But it seems impossible to reconcile this element with the purely logical development of his speculative system. Cf. Norman Smith's *Studies in the Cartesian Philosophy*, chapter ii. For a searching examination of the whole Cartesian philosophy, reference should be made to the article on " Cartesianism " by Dr. Edward Caird in the ninth edition of the *Encyclopædia Britannica*, reproduced in *Essays on Literature and Philosophy*. See also Adamson's *Development of Modern Philosophy*, Vol. I.

pletely humanistic, in the sense in which that term is here understood. The Platonic elements which he uses cannot but be felt to be somewhat alien in reality to a system the main features of which still retain that purely quantitative aspect which is characteristic of Cartesianism in general. The differences between the monads, for instance, are still explained by Leibniz as differences of degree ; *
and even the idea of final cause is in constant danger of being resolved in practice into a case of mere identity.†

In short, it seems fair to say that the general tendency of the Cartesian philosophy was towards naturalism ; or at least that the inevitable logic of it bore in this direction. Perhaps we might add that the inner spirit of its leading adherents carried them in a very different direction ; and that there is, in consequence, in almost all of them, a continual conflict between the force by which they are carried and the force by which they try to guide themselves. Hence there is always a rift within their lute. Their prevailing naturalism is continually qualified by a thin vein of humanism ; starting from the thinking ego of Descartes—" o ame ! o esprit ! "

---

* Cf. the later doctrine of Kant, with whom degree is the scheme of quality.   See below, Lecture IX.

† Cf. Caird, *Critical Philosophy of Kant*, Vol. I, p. 98.

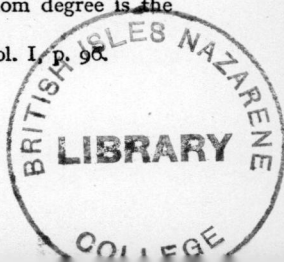

as Gassendi addressed him—running through the Spinozistic "imagination," * and showing itself in his fine ethical aspirations, and culminating at last in the Leibnizian realm of ends. But they are never really able to shake themselves free from the slough of naturalism which is inevitably bound up with their mathematical method.

The naturalism of the prevailing British school of thought at the corresponding period is still more pronounced; though this also is qualified by the vein of idealism which shows itself especially in the philosophy of Berkeley. One might imagine, indeed, at first, from the prevailingly psychological tone of English speculation, that its tendencies were eminently humanistic. But the psychological tendency grew primarily out of the philosophy of Hobbes, and continued to be coloured by that strongly naturalistic source. The activity of thought, the ends by which it is directed, even the feeling that guides it, tend to sink into the background, and the mind is thought of primarily as mirroring an

* It seems hardly too much to say that, if Spinoza had ever developed his doctrine of imagination in a really positive fashion, instead of a merely negative and critical way, his point of view would have become almost indistinguishable from that of Leibniz. As it is, his work is of course immensely superior to that of Leibniz, from the point of view of ethics and politics ; but it is difficult to reconcile his treatment of these subjects with his rejection of teleology in metaphysics.

external world, in relation to which it is almost purely passive and receptive. Locke does indeed speak of the mind as active ; but it is not easy to discover what it does, except connect together the materials that it passively receives ; and it is easy for subsequent philosophers to urge that, from this point of view, we may very well suppose that the materials are quite well able to connect themselves, without the intervention of any special subjective activity. Accordingly, the outcome of Locke's line of thought is seen, in the end, in the pure associationism of Hume, according to which the interaction of mental elements is conceived in a quite mechanical fashion. Self, with its unity, its ends, its activities, its independent individuality, has completely disappeared ; and we are left with a thoroughly naturalistic interpretation of human nature.

Berkeley, of course, fought hard against this ; just as Malebranche, Spinoza, and Leibniz contended against the naturalistic current of Cartesianism. But the river-gods were in both cases too strong for the resisting heroes ; the stream of tendency carried them on in spite of themselves ; though it cannot, by any means, be granted that their efforts were entirely futile. They prepared the way for Kant and those subsequent idealists by whom a more or less solidly based humanism was at length established.

The " Copernican revolution " of Kant was a movement in opposition both to the Cartesian and to the Lockeian lines of development ; and in a certain sense it was opposed to both in the same way. Both were primarily attempts to interpret human knowledge as the apprehension, by the way of "ideas," of a world that is in its nature independent of the mind that knows it. Kant urges that we should try whether a better account cannot be given of knowledge by recognizing at the outset that the mind can only know what it in a manner makes for itself, and consequently that the world which is presented to man must be an essentially human world—a world conforming to the modes of his mental life. It is from this humanistic point of view that the Kantian philosophy is constructed throughout. Accordingly, we find that the humanistic conceptions of quality, end, purpose, and the like, play a conspicuous part in his speculative constructions. The world, as he conceives it, is to be anthropocentrically interpreted. But this is subject to some rather large qualifications. The categories of quality and end, for instance, do not by any means have full scope in his treatment. Quality, indeed, is reduced to a species of quantity ;

the conception of end has a very subordinate place in the ethics ; and in the *Critique of Judgment* it is treated as only a regulative conception.* This is partly due to the fact that Kant did not really escape from the limitations of the previous philosophical methods, and partly to the very unfortunate way in which he arrived at his list of categories. Moreover, the humanism of his point of view is in the end fatally limited by the conception of the " Thing-in-itself," as lying quite beyond the grasp of the human intelligence. Still, with all these qualifications, and even with some others that might be added, it remains true that Kant did much to establish the general position which I am here describing as humanism upon a firm scientific basis.

The later German idealists sought, in general, to escape from the limitations of the Kantian system, and to make his doctrine more emphatically humanistic. This is true in particular of Fichte and Hegel. Hegel especially represents an almost complete humanism. His final interpretation of the world is in the light of the development of "spirit"; and by " spirit " he means the evolution of the human consciousness. Even his humanism, however, is

* For some further comments on these points see the Supplementary Lecture at the end of this volume.

perhaps somewhat qualified by the fact that he
tends to subordinate feeling and will to the more
purely cognitive side of experience—an inheritance,
in the main, from the Cartesian school.*   It is also
qualified to some extent by the fact that, while
treating of the development of the human consciousness, he professes to regard it from the point
of view of " the Absolute."   This is, however, not
much of a qualification ;   since it is of the essence
of his doctrine that there is in the end no real distinction between the human point of view and that
of the Absolute.   But it does to some extent prevent
his doctrine from being a humanism in the narrower
sense.   The full significance of this will become
more apparent as we proceed.

Although representing a very different point of
view, the humanism of Comte has really a close connection with that of the German idealists.   It
differs chiefly in being a pure humanism, definitely
placing human life on a footing of its own, over
against any attempt to interpret the world of
nature.   It thus leaves naturalism—or at least a
naturalistic agnosticism—in possession of the larger
half of the universe ;   and contents itself with

---

* The point has, however, often been very greatly exaggerated ; for intelligence, as Hegel conceives it, is certainly purposive. Still, it is probably true that this aspect of it is hardly
made sufficiently explicit.

maintaining that human life is to be regarded in a different way. Humanity, for Comte, is the Great Being which alone is worthy of our worship and devotion, a real unity developing towards the highest and noblest ends. The world of nature has value and significance only in so far as man uses it for his own purposes. The heavens declare, not the glory of God, but the glory of Kepler, Galileo, and Newton, or rather the glory of that great God Humanity, of whose life these famous men were organs and expressions. This is a humanism of a narrower type, and at the same time less purely intellectual in its tendencies, than that represented by German idealism.

If we were considering at all fully the development of modern speculative thought, it would be necessary to add here some further reference to one or two of the post-Kantian metaphysicians, such as Fichte and Schopenhauer, who both laid special emphasis on the place of will. Fichte is, indeed, more particularly interesting, from our present point of view, on account of the way in which he applied his philosophical conceptions to the treatment of political and sociological questions.* But I cannot here do more

---

* Fichte has also a special interest for English readers, on account of the profound influence which his ideas had on Carlyle, perhaps the most potent of our recent humanists.

than allude to these writers. I may note, however, in connection with them that the meaning of humanism that has been most prominently brought forward in recent times is characterized by a similar emphasis on the will. Professor James and others have urged upon us the importance of recognizing that, even in our most purely theoretical investigations, we are constantly guided by the idea of an end ; and that what we call truth is consequently not to be regarded as something purely statical, but is always of the nature of the realization of a human ideal. This view must certainly be regarded as one illustration of what I here understand by humanism.

In illustrating what I understand by a humanistic movement in thought, both in this lecture and in the previous one, I have of course referred almost exclusively to definitely philosophical lines of thought. It would be easy no doubt to illustrate similar tendencies in the more general expressions of human thought that are to be found in literature. Poetic literature, in particular, constantly reflects the higher significance of the thought of the age in which it appears ; and it is especially sensitive to any changes in men's ideas about human life. Though Matthew Arnold's description of poetry as " criticism of life " is not wholly satisfactory, yet it seems at least true to say that all the really great poetry of the world is concerned with the interpretation of human life. Hence poetry tends to appear at its highest in those ages in which humanistic conceptions are most strongly prevalent. The development of humanism among the Greeks was accompanied by the growth of a great poetic literature, in which ideas about life were impressively and significantly set forth. The humanism of the Renaissance shows itself in a similar European literature, culminating in the Elizabethan drama. The modern period in which naturalism specially prevailed presents, on the other hand, a relatively prosaic appearance.* We tend, for instance, to get a pure nature-poetry like that of Thomson's "Seasons," or analytical accounts of human life, like those that are given us by Pope, in which the actions of men and women are accounted for by "ruling passions" and other mechanical devices. Again, the more idealistic conceptions that have begun to prevail once again in more recent times have been accompanied by the growth of a poetic literature, in which the interpretation of human life has become increasingly dominant. We might, for

* It should be noted, however, that one of the greatest of Roman poets, Lucretius, is a leading exponent of naturalism. The Romans, indeed, in general went further than perhaps any other people in turning brute force and the external machinery of life into a kind of poetry, and almost into a kind of religion.

E

instance, from this point of view, contrast the general attitude towards life that is adopted by Wordsworth and Shelley with that taken by Browning. For Shelley nature seems a higher and, one might almost say, a more spiritual being than man. Human life almost appears sometimes to be regarded as if it were a blot on creation.

> " Life, like a dome of many-coloured glass,
>   Stains the white radiance of Eternity."

Yet the poet of *Prometheus Unbound* was certainly at heart a humanist ; and much of the later poetic interpretation of human life can be traced very directly to his influence. For Wordsworth no doubt human life counts, in general, for a good deal more ; but for him also, if there is a " music of humanity," it is apt at least to be somewhat " still " and " sad." In contrast with both these, the buoyant optimism about human life that characterizes Browning is extremely noticeable. For him, indeed, it is the growth of a soul that is alone worth studying. Nature sinks into the background, or is only interesting as the field in which human life is spent. Such differences are no doubt in part traceable to differences of character and temperament and individual experience. It should be remembered also that the " nature " that is revered by Shelley and Wordsworth is not the mechanical system of the mathematical physicist, but a nature imaginatively interpreted as reflecting what is highest in the human consciousness. But, when all such qualifications have been made, it remains true that in poetic thought also we can trace the growth of a new spirit, a tendency to seek in human life for something that is intrinsically deeper, more interesting, more significant, than anything that we can observe in the world around.

These remarks must suffice by way of indicating what I understand by the humanistic movement in ancient and modern thought, in contrast with the naturalistic tendency that went before it. In the lectures that follow it will be my object to try to bring out more definitely the significance of this point of view ; first in relation to the general problems of philosophy, and afterwards in relation to some of the most central problems of social life.

LECTURE III

HUMANISM IN PHILOSOPHY

I HAVE now indicated the general significance
of humanism, as I understand it, and have
sketched the growth of the philosophical ideas on
which it depends, both in ancient and in modern
times. It is of course not possible in such lectures
as these to discuss, with any thoroughness, the
ultimate metaphysical implications of such a
humanistic position ; * but it is my object in this
lecture to bring out its chief philosophical bearings,
in close relation to the lines of development that
have already been traced.

Though it is perhaps true that the finest and
most characteristic expression of a humanistic
position is to be found in ancient Greece, yet in some
respects the modern line of development is even
more remarkable, and, for our present purpose, more
instructive ; and it may be most profitable to consider its significance mainly in relation to the latter.

* This is, however, a little more fully attempted in the
Supplementary Lecture at the end of this course.

Both the naturalism and the humanism of ancient times were less definitely formed ; and they do not yield as clear an antithesis as we find in more modern lines of thought. Plato's humanism, for instance, was a good deal qualified by the geometrical character of his fundamental conceptions ; and even so staunch a humanist as Aristotle is constrained to allow that human life is but a poor thing in comparison with that of the heavenly bodies.* In contrast with such limitations, the humanism of such moderns as Hegel and Comte, if less free and natural, seems in many respects more thorough and whole-hearted. This is probably due in the main to the fact that the position of naturalism has become more sharply defined ; and that its opposition to humanism has thus become more clearly apparent.

The development of the natural sciences in modern times has given a meaning to nature, as an ordered and connected system, governed by inviolable laws, which it did not possess at all in ancient times, even in the minds of the founders of the natural sciences themselves. The increasing freedom of the moral and political life—the original provinces of the reign of "law" †—has also tended

---

* *Nicomachean Ethics*, Book VI, chapter VII.

† i.e. of νόμος, as opposed to φύσις. It is, I believe, true to say that the conception of "laws of nature" was practi-

further to emphasize the distinction between the
purposive person and the mechanically driven
thing. Even the increasing dominance of material
conditions in modern times has perhaps tended to
make us feel more keenly the contrast between the
instruments and circumstances of life and life itself.
When Emerson tells us—

> " 'Tis the day of the chattel,
>   Web to weave and corn to grind;
>   Things are in the saddle,
>   And ride mankind,"

we probably feel the sting of the antithesis as no
ancient could have felt it. It is largely on account
of the increasing sharpness of this contrast that both
naturalism and humanism have acquired a significance for us that they could hardly have possessed
at any earlier period.

Naturalism, in its most modern sense, has been
made possible by that definite conception of the
system of the physical universe which has been
slowly built up by the natural sciences, aided by
certain philosophical conceptions derived in the
main, I think we may fairly say, from the ancient
atomists and the modern Cartesians. The physical
universe has thus come to be thought of as the sphere

tically unknown to ancient thought until the time of the Stoics;
and that it was introduced by them primarily as an ethical
rather than a physical conception.

of matter and motion, interpreted by means of purely mechanical determinations. Over against this we have the realm of life and thought, to which definiteness has been given by the growth of the biological sciences, and still more by the development of that subjective standpoint which is associated with the doubt of Descartes and with introspective psychology. Man, in particular, has in this way come to be thought of as a microcosm, a little universe within himself, requiring to be interpreted in a quite peculiar way.

Now, as I have already indicated, what chiefly gives significance to this antithesis between the human and the natural, or between the vital and the mechanical, is the presence of elements that require or suggest a teleological interpretation in the former, and the absence of such elements in the latter. The fundamental idea of humanism I take to be that of end or purpose. It is in virtue of this that man has a history, in the distinctive sense that was previously referred to, and it is this that gives him a unique position in nature. In Plato's way of putting it, he is governed by the idea of the good ; or, in Kantian phrase, he guides himself by the conception of law. All that is specially distinctive of man—his freedom, his morality, his progress—connects directly with this peculiarity, which seems

to make him, indeed, almost a miracle in nature.
As Goethe expresses it—

> " Man alone can perform the impossible ;
> He distinguishes, chooses, and judges ;
> He can impart to the moment duration." *

But it is hardly possible for science or for philosophy
to treat this peculiarity of man's life simply as a
miracle. What we have to ask, consequently, is
really this—What is the place of the idea of end or
purpose in a philosophical theory of the world ?
This is a question, of course, that cannot be adequately discussed in such a lecture as this ; but I
must try to bring out what appear to me to be the
main bearings of the problem.

Historically, as we know, the idea of final cause
is, in the first instance, traceable to Anaxagoras,
who seemed to Aristotle like a sober man among
those who idly babbled, because he appeared to
explain the universe by reference to a purpose,
instead of the blind elemental forces of the earlier
philosophers. The way in which this introduction
of purpose impressed some contemporary thinkers
is strikingly brought out by Plato in a well-known
passage in the *Phædo*, which I may here recall to

* " Nur allein der mensch
   Vermag das Unmögliche ;
   Er unterscheidet,
   Wählet, und richtet ;
   Er kann dem Augenblick Dauer verleihen."

your minds : " Then I heard some one who had a
book of Anaxagoras, as he said, out of which he read
that mind was the disposer and cause of all, and I
was quite delighted at this notion, which appeared
admirable, and I said to myself : If mind is the disposer, mind will dispose all for the best, and put
each particular in the best place ; and I argued that
if any one desired to find out the cause of the generation or destruction or existence of anything, he
must find out what state of being or suffering or
doing was best for that thing, and therefore a man
had only to consider the best for himself and others,
and then he would also know the worse, for that the
same science comprised both. And I rejoiced to
think that I had found in Anaxagoras a teacher of
the causes of existence such as I desired, and I
imagined that he would tell me first whether the
earth is flat or round ; and then he would further
explain the cause and the necessity of this, and
would teach me the nature of the best and show
that this was best ; and if he said that the earth was
in the centre, he would explain that this position was
the best, and I should be satisfied with the explanation given, and not want any other sort of
cause. And I thought that I would then go on and
ask him about the sun and moon and stars, and that
he would explain to me their comparative swiftness,

and their returnings and various states, active and passive, and how all of them were for the best.   For I could not imagine that when he spoke of mind as the disposer of them, he would give any other account of their being as they are, except that this was best, and I thought that when he had explained to me in detail the cause of each and the cause of all, he would go on to explain to me what was best for each and what was best for all. . . . What hopes I had formed, and how grievously was I disappointed ! As I proceeded, I found my philosopher altogether forsaking mind or any other principle of order, and having recourse to air, and ether, and water, and other eccentricities. I might compare him to a person who began by maintaining generally that mind is the cause of the actions of Socrates, but who, when he endeavoured to explain the causes of my several actions in detail, went on to show that I sit here because my body is made up of bones and muscles ; and the bones, as he would say, are hard and have joints which divide them, and the muscles are elastic, and they cover the bones, which have also a covering or environment of flesh and skin which contains them ; and as the bones are lifted at their joints by the contraction or relaxation of the muscles, I am able to bend my limbs, and this is why I am sitting here in a curved posture ; this is what he would say, and he would have a similar explanation of my talking to you, which he would attribute to sound, and air, and hearing, and he would assign ten thousand other causes of the same sort, forgetting to mention the true cause, which is, that the Athenians have thought fit to condemn me, and accordingly I have thought it better and more right to remain here and undergo my sentence ; for I am inclined to think that these muscles and bones of mine would have gone off long ago to Megara or Bœotia—by the dog of Egypt they would, if they had been moved only by their own idea of what was best, and if I had not chosen as the better and nobler part, instead of playing truant and running away, to undergo any punishment which the state inflicts."

Here you have the contrast between naturalism and humanism in its simplest and most primitive form, the contrast between the explanation of things by purpose, on the analogy of human action, and their explanation by the analysis of their physical conditions. And of course we know that, in view of this contrast, Plato entirely and Aristotle mainly adopted throughout their philosophy the humanistic method of explanation.

The earlier philosophers, on the other hand, were content with material causes ; and modern philo-

sophy, as represented by the Cartesians, came round
again, as we have seen, to a similar position.   Bacon
also, while commending the use of final causes from
the theological point of view, regrets that, in the
finite sphere at any rate, teleology, " like a virgin
consecrated to God," produces nothing.   Now, it
would seem that modern scientific inquiry has
tended, more and more, to follow along this line.
In pure physics or chemistry or astronomy no one
thinks of inquiring into the purpose for which
phenomena have been arranged in a particular order.
The regular sequence of events is all that really
comes into consideration.   The biological sciences
were no doubt somewhat slower in abandoning
teleological considerations ; but the last stronghold,
it might seem, of teleological explanation was over-
thrown when the modern theory of evolution was
introduced and established.   The idea of the
" struggle for existence " and of the " survival of
the fittest " (which means only of the fittest to survive) is certainly as naturalistic as it could well be.
And it is in the same direction that all the natural
sciences would appear to be steadily moving.   Indeed, flushed by the successes which they have in
various directions won, the naturalists have even
ventured to invade the provinces of ethics and social
philosophy, and to maintain that even the facts of

human life can be explained without any teleological interpretations.

Now, there can be very little question that, for purposes of scientific analysis, this rejection of final causes is fully justified, and is even absolutely necessary. The question is rather, whether it is right for purposes of ultimate philosophical inter-pretation. The distinction between these two points of view is one that has constantly tended to come up in the development of human thought, and that has recently begun once more to be recog-nized. It is perhaps almost equivalent to the old Parmenidean antithesis between the Way of Opinion and the Way of Truth, and certainly it is not far removed from the distinction between science and philosophy that was introduced by Plato, partially revived by Leibniz, and reaffirmed in our own time by F. H. Bradley and many others. Recently, for instance, the distinction has been on the whole very happily illustrated by one who may well be claimed as having distinguished himself both in science and in philosophy, Principal Lloyd Morgan, in his little book on *The Interpretation of Nature*. I do not say that the form in which this distinction has been put forward, whether by Parmenides, by Plato, by Leibniz, by Bradley, or by Lloyd Morgan, can be altogether vindicated ; nor can I well be

expected to discuss here the precise form in which
it is legitimate.* I only urge that, in some form
or other, it is necessary to recognize it ; and that on
this basis we may maintain that, for purposes of
purely scientific analysis, it is right to omit the
humanistic point of view—i.e. to reject teleological
considerations ; but that, for purposes of philosophical interpretation, these considerations are all
important. I hope to make it clearer as I proceed
how it is possible to recognize the legitimacy of two
such apparently opposite modes of explanation ;
but in the meantime I must content myself with
some rather general and perhaps somewhat vague
considerations.

My general meaning may, I think, be sufficiently
explained by reference to the problem of the development of life. It is for biologists to say what the
scientific explanation of the various forms of life
really is ; and I am aware that there are still some
differences of opinion ; but let it be assumed that, in
general language, the " struggle for existence " is at
any rate the explanation of the survival of certain
variations—whatever may be the explanation of these
variations themselves. Then, what I urge is that, while
this may be a perfectly valid and even—what is more

---

* This is, however, a little more fully indicated in Lecture
VIII, and in the Supplementary Lecture at the end.

doubtful—for ordinary scientific purposes, a perfectly complete explanation, it may yet be true that the real meaning of the development of forms of life is to be found in the gradual realization of higher types.

Of course, if this is the case, it must mean that the scientific explanation is not really complete ; but its incompleteness may lie in the ignoring of conditions which it would be quite impossible for any particular science to take into account. In order to bring this out, a few remarks must now be made on the general nature of scientific explanation. For further light on this point I may refer to the very thorough inquiry into the methods of scientific investigation contained in the first volume of Dr. Ward's Gifford Lectures on *Naturalism and Agnosticism*. It is not possible for me to do more than call attention to some leading points.

When final causes are eliminated from scientific inquiry, it is apt to be supposed at first that efficient causes take their place—i.e. that things and events are explained by antecedent modes of existence that possess some inherent power of producing these things and events. This is the view that we find at first put forward within the Cartesian school. Every effect is supposed to be due to some cause adequate to produce it—some cause, in fact, which may be said already to contain the effect, either formally or eminently, i.e. as it would appear to mean, either in the same form or in a qualitatively superior form. But, as I have already indicated, qualitative superiority soon ceases to have any meaning in the Cartesian school, and in the methods of modern scientific analysis in general. As soon as this is recognized, the efficiency of causation is seen to mean nothing but that the effect is already contained in the cause. If this were pressed to its ultimate issue, it would mean that nothing really happens at all. If the effect is contained completely within the cause, there is no real change. This result was, of course, accepted in the ancient Parmenidean philosophy, and it seems to be practically involved also in the philosophy of Spinoza. From this point of view, efficient causes are removed quite as completely as final causes ; and the only mode of explanation that is left is that by means of the logical ground—i.e. in the end, the explanation by simple analysis, or by means of the principle of identity.

But modern science does not, in general, press things quite so far as this. It is satisfied with the elimination of ends and qualitative differences from its modes of explanation, and the reduction of all distinctions, so far as it has to deal with them, to distinctions of quantity. Forms change, it is recognized ; but what is maintained by modern science—as by Descartes—is that in all changes the quantity of motion is uniform. Descartes formulated this principle somewhat vaguely and inexactly, treating it as following from the constancy of the divine nature, and not being quite clear as to the precise way in which quantity of motion ought to be estimated. In the modern doctrine of the conservation of energy it is formulated more precisely and proved more rigorously by reference to facts of actual observation. But however it may be formulated, and however it may be proved, the great question remains—What does it really mean for us ? Does it mean that there are in reality no qualitative differences ? Or, if not, what explanation is to be given in connection with it of the occurrence of such differences in the world that we know ?

The general answer would seem to be for modern science—as for Descartes—that in the purely physical world, at any rate, no such differences can be recognized. They must be referred to the inner world of consciousness. Heat, light, sound, and other apparent phenomena of the physical universe are, from the purely material point of view, nothing more than certain modes of motion—ways in which " non-matter in motion " displays itself

F

to our senses.* / In themselves they are merely motion, and the actual quantity of motion does not change. It is only for consciousness that they have those distinctive qualities by which we are affected.

The position, then, amounts to this. If we regard the world without us as a purely mechanical system, all the qualities and ends that enter into our experience have to be referred to our own inner consciousness ; and we have then to ask, What is the nature of the experience with which we are there confronted ? What we seem to find there is a system of forward-looking tendencies, guided throughout by qualitative distinctions. Our very existence as conscious beings would seem to lie in our going on.† Now, it is possible, no doubt, to give a quasi-naturalistic turn even to this aspect of our conscious life. Spinoza, for instance, describes it as a *conatus in suo esse perseverandi*, and so might seem to bring it into direct relation to the inertia by which all

* If we take the view of Descartes, that the material system has no characteristics but those that are strictly spatial, even motion seems to become meaningless, except as a change in the way in which some conscious being is affected. But modern physics conceives of matter as something in space, though something to which, in itself, no definite qualities can be ascribed. The qualities attributed to it are merely descriptions of the way in which it behaves.

† This conative aspect of all conscious process is very fully brought out by modern psychologists. See, for instance, Stout's *Manual*.

physical masses seem to be characterized. But the great point of difference—which certainly Spinoza's way of looking at it tends to obscure—is that the constant forward-looking movement of the human consciousness is dependent on a more or less conscious apprehension of qualitative differences in the content that comes before it, and on a more or less explicit choice of the better. But, it may be said, we speak also of attractions and natural affinities among the objects that are without us. The point, however, is that, if nature is to be interpreted in a purely mechanical fashion, such attractions and affinities are as purely metaphorical as the φιλία and νεῖκος of Empedocles. And the point is, further, that where real qualitative differences are apprehended and become the explanation of movement, attraction and affinity cease to be merely metaphorical. Indeed, to say that one thing is qualitatively different from another seems to mean nothing at all unless it implies that they influence things differently, and in a way that cannot be explained by purely quantitative distinctions. Now such qualitative action is excluded by the strictly mechanical interpretation of nature. But such qualitative action is what we are constantly aware of in our own conscious life ; and indeed it may be said to be the only kind of action of which we have any real knowledge.

Are we to say, then, that qualitative differences, and the movements that depend upon them, belong exclusively to our life as conscious beings ? According to this view, consciousness is indeed a wonder-working faculty, a constant miracle in nature, creating a world of qualitative differences which is nowhere else to be found. This difficulty is partly concealed in the Cartesian system, by the ascription of this miraculous agency, first to the composite nature of man, and afterwards to God. The former of these solutions is soon seen to be inconsistent with the complete separation between mind and body, which is pre-supposed in the statement of the problem. The latter solution, on the other hand, is either an abandonment of the problem —if we mean by God simply an unintelligible being by whom this miracle is performed—or else it must be taken to mean that the creation of qualitative differences is to be explained by some sort of mental activity. Mental activity, in fact, becomes, on this view, the only ultimate explanation of any change, and so the only real cause that is anywhere to be found.*

But this is a result which it is not easy to accept, from the point of view of the scientific interpretation

* This seems to be the view that is suggested in Ward's *Naturalism and Agnosticism.* It is also the view of Berkeley and his modern disciples—e.g. Dr. Rashdall in his recent *Theory of Good and Evil.*

of the universe. It seems clear, from obvious facts of experience, that the human mind does not itself create the qualitative differences which it apprehends. We cannot make for ourselves a single sensible quality, but appear obviously to be entirely dependent for these upon the receptivity of our senses. And to say that such qualities may be created by another mind than ours, by an infinite or divine mind, and communicated to ours—say, in the way of a divine language, such as that expounded by Berkeley—is only to play with words and shelve the problem. A mind which should work in this way would certainly not be such a mind as we have any knowledge or conception of. Further, the way in which the mind grows up in connection with the body, and the way in which the two appear to interact, makes it almost impossible to sever the two in this absolute fashion, in any real attempt to account for the facts of life. Hence it is not surprising that those who have been in some measure forced to recognize a distinction between the two on such grounds as have been indicated, and have yet tried to work out a systematic view of the universe, have generally had recourse to the doctrine of psycho-physical parallelism. They have held, that is to say, that, in spite of their apparent diversity—a diversity so great as to make any real interaction impossible—they have yet an underlying identity. The most thorough form of this doctrine is the Spinozistic theory of one substance with two completely corresponding aspects ; but it is often held in a somewhat looser and vaguer form.

But it seems clear that this is either a mere evasion of the problem, or else brings up the same problem in a different form. It is a mere evasion if it simply states—and this seems to be all that is meant by some of the psychologists who maintain it—that we have to recognize the fact that mental and material changes take place in a certain orderly and concurrent fashion, but that we must never hope to give any real account of their connection. If it means more than this, it seems simply to bring us back to our original problem. For it is precisely the want of parallelism between the mental and the material that is the crux of the whole difficulty. It is because the one is all quantity—extensive quantity, analysable into actual units—and the other all quality or degree, that no common measure can be found of them. The doctrine of psycho-physical parallelism is, consequently, not much more than an attempt to evade or conceal the difficulty.*

* Some further remarks on this point will be found in Lecture VIII.

In the end, there seems to be no escape from this difficulty, except by the frank recognition that quality and degree, as well as extensive quantity, are elements in the universe of which we are trying to give an explanation or interpretation ; and that any kind of explanation which is only capable of dealing with quantity must be regarded as quite incomplete.

The question, then, remains—How are qualitative differences to be dealt with ? Now, it seems clear that they cannot possibly be reduced to quantitative differences. We can find a " mechanical equivalent " of heat or of any other quality that we apprehend ; but no amount of heaping up of units will ever turn the thing that we experience as heat into the thing that we experience as sound, or reduce any quality that we know into any other, or even any degree of a quality that we know into any other degree of it. It cannot, then, be by any method of quantitative analysis that qualities are to be explained. Shall we, then, try to explain them by means of efficient causes ? But efficient causes seem, as we have seen, to mean nothing in the end but that the effect is already contained in the cause. The origin of any quality, therefore, cannot be accounted for in this way. What method of explanation, then, are we to adopt ? Or are we to give up all explanation as hopeless ?

It is such questions as these that bring us back to the conception of final cause. It was indeed such considerations that led Leibniz to reintroduce teleology into his interpretation of the universe. Unfortunately, he did this in a somewhat fantastic form *—a form that has led his philosophy to be characterized as "a fairy-tale of speculation"—and it was gradually whittled away by his successors, till even with Kant it had hardly any positive significance. What is wanted in philosophy, now, is to reintroduce the conception, without these fantastic elements.

But, it may be asked, how can we ever hope that final causes can be, by themselves, a real method of explanation ? Does not a final cause simply mean an end or purpose ? And does not the pursuit of an end or purpose presuppose a being who actively sets that end before himself, and efficiently seeks to carry it out ? Does not a final cause, therefore,

---

* This fantastic form is no doubt partly intentional on the part of Leibniz, and is adopted in imitation of the mythological method of Plato. But, as with Plato, it is difficult to remove the myth, without at the same time removing the meaning. It may be added, however, that the real obstacle in the way of any really fruitful use of the principle of final causation by Leibniz lies in the fact that he has no real place for qualitative differences; and without some distinction between higher and lower, better and worse, there seems to be no meaning in an end. In spite of the attempt to introduce final causes, his fundamental position remains mathematical, rather than ethical.

lead us back to an efficient cause ? This is a speculative problem, which cannot be very satisfactorily dealt with in such a lecture as this ; but I may briefly indicate what appears to me to be the answer.* When we say that we set ourselves to achieve an end or carry out a purpose, what happens is—(1) that something presents itself to us as a good ; (2) that we " identify ourselves " with this end, i.e. that it fits into the general system of our conception of good on the whole ; (3) that, as a result of this, certain organic adjustments begin to take place. These organic adjustments, so far as they are simply physical facts, take place in accordance with the general laws of material phenomena, i.e.

---

* I am, of course, here touching, necessarily in a very summary and inadequate fashion, upon one of the most thorny problems of psychological analysis. The discussion in *Mind* by Mr. F. H. Bradley and Professor Ward represent two strikingly antagonistic views on the subject ; and the more recent attempts by such experimental psychologists as Professor Titchener to eliminate the element of activity from consciousness are also deserving of attention. One of the latest, and I think one of the best, attempts to deal with the subject is that by Professor Stout in the *British Journal of Psychology* for July, 1906. The essential point seems to be that we must recognize an element in consciousness distinct from presentation and feeling ; but that this element is not properly to be regarded as a consciousness of efficiency or action, but rather of what we may describe as a forward-looking tendency. I return to this point in the Supplementary Lecture at the end ; but I cannot, of course, hope to deal with it in anything like an adequate way in such a course of lectures as this.

there is transference of motion, but no real creation
or loss. The end or purpose—the recognition of
something as for us a good—would seem here to be
the real explanation of the change that takes place ;
and it may be doubted whether we have any real
reason, in the end, to look for any other kind of
explanation. What I mean is that the recognition
of something as good, or congruent with the life of
the self, is the same thing as a conscious movement
towards it ; and that this conscious movement is
the only explanation that is really required for the
accompanying bodily movements. Bodily movements, from the point of view of modern physical
science, are only explicable by the general nature
of the physical system, and especially by the continuity of its modes of motion. That the choice of
the better should be one of the modes in which this
motion is directed, without alteration in its quantity,
seems in no way incompatible with the harmony of
the physical system.

Now, what I am seeking to emphasize here is that,
if this view is to be adopted, it means that the explanation is by a final cause, something apprehended as better, rather than by anything of the
nature of a *vis a tergo*. If once we admit the legitimacy of such a mode of explanation, we are certainly
not far removed from such a point of view as that of

Plato, according to whom the Idea of the Good is the ultimate principle of all philosophical interpretation. To allow this, however, is at the same time to maintain that there are qualitative differences in the universe, that some things are really better than others, and not merely preferable for particular individuals. To interpret the universe in this way is what I understand by a humanistic interpretation.

This, you may say, is not only humanism, but even voluntarism, and that of a rather extreme type. I think, at any rate, it is not quite what is commonly understood by that term. Voluntarism is generally taken to imply the affirmation of the individual will as an independently acting force, standing apart from that on which it operates. It is conceived as a special activity within our conscious life, and again as an operative principle within the life of the universe. Now, it is certainly difficult to reconcile such an affirmation with the unity that we seem to find both in our consciousness and in the system of the world. Moreover, in seeking to explain one aspect of our experience, it leaves another more unintelligible than ever. It explains the bare fact of choice, or rather bids us accept it as an unaccountable activity ; but it fails to explain the existence of those qualitative distinctions which alone give significance to the act of choice. The view, on the other hand, that I am trying here to set before you, explains these two aspects of our experience together. The recognition of qualitative differences is at the same time the choice of one as against another ; for recognized differences are probably never entirely indifferent to us. At any rate, when differences are such that one is recognized as fitting in with the growing life of the conscious being, that one is selected as against others. The activity is thus conceived, not as something apart from the conscious life of the individual, but simply as that life itself in its growing unity, as distinguished from the changing content with which it is concerned. For a conscious being, according to this view, to be alive is to apprehend differences and choose between them. And the corresponding view with regard to the universe in general is that it contains real differences, by which its growth is guided or explained. The will in the individual and the final cause in the universe are, on this interpretation, not something apart from the individual and the universe, but simply express the fact that they are alive. The finality, in the language of metaphysicians, is immanent. It simply means that there is a real process in the life of the being to which it is applied. The recognition of this is certainly not what is commonly understood by voluntarism.

The conceptions at which I have thus briefly and summarily hinted are no doubt of a difficult and highly speculative character ; and, as it is not the primary object of this course to discuss either psychological or metaphysical problems, I must not at present pursue them further. What I have sought to bring out is merely that the naturalistic point of view, when pushed to its extreme limits, either leaves us with no intelligible explanation of the ultimate facts of our experience or points us over to an interpretation which is in reality humanistic. If this is not enough to justify us in endeavouring to treat the universe as a whole on a humanistic basis—a large and daring enterprise— it may at least serve as some excuse for the attempt to regard human life itself from the point of view of purpose and qualitative difference.

At any rate, what I have attempted in this introductory part of the course, has been to set sharply before you the contrast between these two fundamental points of view—the mechanical system of nature and the human realm of ends—as they appear both in ancient and in modern thought ; and to indicate how it is that naturalism seems to fail us, if not in dealing with the universe as a whole, or in dealing with the material system itself, at least in the effort to interpret human life. Whether the treatment by reference to ends and qualitative differences can itself be made finally satisfactory, it is not really possible to discuss within the limits of such a course as this.* What I have said may suffice at least to indicate what I mean by it, and to show why it is that I describe it as a humanistic mode of explanation, in contrast with the naturalistic mode of explanation, which is adopted by the purely physical sciences, and in contrast also with the idea of efficient cause, which leads in the direction of supernaturalism.

Having given these general explanations of what I understand by humanism as a philosophical doctrine, I may now proceed, in the lectures that follow, to give some account of certain results that seem to me to follow from the adoption of a humanistic point of view in the treatment of several of the most important aspects of life, and in this way illustrate the sociological bearings of the subject.

* I have, however, attempted this to some extent in the Supplementary Lecture.

LECTURE IV

HUMANISM IN POLITICS

HOWEVER true it may be that the universe can in the end only be interpreted in the light of purpose, it is certain that it would be extremely difficult to trace such purpose in nature ; and it must probably be allowed that, for the purposes of ordinary scientific analysis, it ought to be rigidly excluded. If it is the " way of truth," it is at any rate not the way of sound " opinion " in scientific investigation. But, if so, if may be urged that for all the ordinary purposes of life it must be almost meaningless. If all exact science is quantitative, what place is there left for the study of quality and purpose ? To this the most obvious answer is that at any rate in the study of human life itself these elements retain a place. In the world around us there are distinguishable qualities ; but it seems impossible, or at any rate very difficult, to give any precise account of their relations to one another. There are, it would seem, degrees of excellence ;

but it is not easy to show that there is any definite preference for the higher as against the lower.* It is only human beings who definitely recognize merit, and tend to side with the better. Hence human life seems to demand to be studied in a somewhat different way from that in which we commonly, and perhaps rightly, study the world of nature.

Indeed, even in human life, it is sometimes apt to appear as if quality and purpose had but a small part to play. When " fortune favours fools " and " the wicked flourish like the green bay tree," human life seems to be almost as blindly determined as that of unthinking nature; and even when wisdom and goodness appear triumphant, it is often not by any means apparent that their success is a result of conscious forethought. Human beings seem, at any rate, often to set out from the point of view of animal instinct ; and they seldom build well, except when they are building better than they know. Even the supreme heroes—the sages, poets, prophets, rulers—appear often to be guided by a power not their own, and to be in the end little more than flies on the wheel of progress. Hence it has some-

* Recent tendencies in the biological sciences, however, would seem to indicate that the conception of a distinction between higher and lower may in the future play a more prominent part in these studies.

times been thought that, even in the scientific interpretation of human life, the conception of any definite purpose or self-conscious end may be safely eliminated.

The early Greek philosophers, as I have already indicated, did not exempt human life from the general naturalism of their treatment. They tended to regard man, to adopt Huxley's phrase, as being little more than " the cunningest of nature's clocks." Nor, when some of the sophists emphasized the distinction between φύσις and νόμος, and so sepaseparated off the study of human life to some extent from that of natural phenomena, can this be in any way regarded as placing human life on a higher level, but rather as introducing a doubt with regard to the possibility of its scientific treatment. Socrates sought to remove this doubt by representing the treatment of human life as an art rather than a science, and so as dependent on the conception of an end; and it was along this line that the humanistic treatment of ethics and politics was developed; even the Aristotelian method in these subjects bearing decided traces of this limitation.*

Apart from this line of growth, the nearest

---

* This point is forcibly brought out in Caird's *Evolution of Theology in the Greek Philosophers*, Lecture XI, where the limitation is possibly a little exaggerated.

G

approach to a scientific treatment of human life in ancient times is on a purely naturalistic basis, and is to be traced especially in the development of the conception of a " social contract." We find an early indication of this doctrine near the beginning of Plato's *Republic*. The view is there brought forward that the social virtues (for so we may render δικαιοσυνή) are not based on any internal end or ideal within the man who practises them, but on the interest of the stronger party in the state. And a contract is represented as having been entered into at the formation of human society, with a view to securing the interest of the stronger. This doctrine has been more fully developed, in a somewhat modified form, by some modern writers, and especially by Hobbes ; and it may be regarded as the most strictly naturalistic interpretation of the life of the state. According to this view, the development of human life is not to be explained by its inner purpose, but by a struggle for existence—or for " power," as Hobbes puts it—among contending forces.

Another interpretation of human life that may in the main be described as naturalistic, is that which rests on Hedonism. This I consider to be less distinctively naturalistic than the theory of the social contract ; since the conception of pleasure is really the conception of a definite human end or good; and it is possible to state a Hedonistic theory—for instance, in the form given by Sidgwick —in a way that can hardly be regarded as naturalistic at all. But in the form in which it has chiefly prevailed in the past, the form in which it has influenced practical legislation, the form in which it has served as a basis for theories of politics and economics, it is almost as purely naturalistic as the doctrine of Hobbes. The form to which I refer is of course that for which Bentham was mainly responsible. This type of Hedonism is, as Sidgwick puts it, psychological; i.e. it is a doctrine of the forces by which individual men are actually governed, quite as much as a theory of their ultimate good or end. It amounts, indeed, to little more than the substitution of the more definite conception of a sum of pleasures for the vague conception of " power " that was chiefly used by Hobbes. There was, no doubt, one other important modification— viz. the introduction of the view that the good at which we are to aim is the " greatest happiness of the greatest number." This modifies the conception of society as a number of warring units; but it still leaves it to be thought of as a sum of disconnected units, whose good is to be separately achieved, and whose efforts after that good may, and probably

will, come into conflict. The conception of human
life as a struggle between individuals, each impelled
by a private inner force, is, consequently, not in
reality greatly altered by the theory of Bentham.
Man's life is not conceived as guided by the thought
of a great ultimate good to be achieved, but rather
as pressed on from behind by a number of inclina-
tions, among which no qualitative differences are
recognized. J. S. Mill, as we all know, tried to
change this conception by the introduction of
qualitative differences among pleasures ; but this
has been generally recognized as an illogical addition
to the Benthamite theory.

The point of view of Bentham is specially important in modern sociology, from the great influence which it has exerted, and which it still
continues to exert, on economic studies ; and from
the fact that it forms the basis of what has been
known as " philosophical radicalism," to which so
many of the ideas of our modern progressive politics
may be traced. On economics I hope to have something more to say in the next lecture. In general
politics the influence of utilitarianism may be seen,
both in the prevalence of the conception of the
general happiness as the great end to be promoted,
and in the absence of any definite conception of any
content for this general happiness, apart from that

which is supplied by individual inclination. It is seen also, more generally, in the view that each is to " count as one," that no qualitative differences are of any real importance, which, consciously or unconsciously, gives so strong a bias to our modern democracy. In this, more than in anything else, we see the essentially naturalistic character of the utilitarian doctrine.

The modern doctrine of evolution brings us to another phase of the naturalism by which all recent thought is so largely tinged. The theory of evolution seems, indeed, at first to be more thoroughly naturalistic than Hedonism ; since the latter points to a conscious end, while the former interprets man's life by reference to an origin in which no human characteristics can be traced. And of some types of the doctrine of evolution this is undoubtedly true. But on the whole the conception of evolution directs us quite as much to the end as to the beginning. It tends, however, to be torn in two directions. On the one hand, it is tempted to explain the end by reference to its origin ; and then it practically ceases to be a true theory of development at all. On the other hand, any attempt to explain the beginning by reference to its ultimate meaning or purpose carries one further into metaphysics than the evolutionist is in general prepared to go. Evolutionism thus on the whole leans to naturalism, but very easily passes over into humanism.

The contrast that I seek to bring out between naturalism and humanism, as applied to politics, is perhaps now sufficiently apparent. During the last age almost everything that could lay claim to a scientific character, at least in this country, was strongly tinged with naturalism. What was chiefly to be opposed to this—apart from the steadily growing influence of Comte and the German idealists—was the emphatic, but not always very clear or coherent, utterances of such writers as Carlyle and Ruskin. Whatever else these writers stand for, they do at any rate put qualitative differences in the forefront, and bring out the need of recognizing purpose in life. At the same time, it must be allowed that Carlyle, and in a lesser degree Ruskin, tend to represent qualitative differences simply as differences of strength or power, and so, after all, to reduce them to a quantitative standard. The purpose of life, moreover, is very vaguely conceived. It seems to be embodied in the insight of the hero or prophet, which is sometimes hardly distinguishable from a blind impulse. And the great doctrine that " right is might," which Carlyle and Ruskin seem to have held in common, passes too readily into the view that " might is right "—if, indeed, the two are logically distinguishable ; * and so becomes an extreme expression of naturalism. To find a genuine humanism, it is almost necessary to go back to the writers by whom these—especially Ruskin— had no doubt been largely influenced, Plato and Aristotle ; though we may also point to other types in Rousseau, Burke, Comte, and in several more recent writers—most of whom, however, have definitely derived a large part of their inspiration from Platonic or Aristotelian sources.

The Platonc doctrine is of course too much wrapped up in parable or myth to be readily available for any direct application to modern life. The sharp division of classes, the elaborate system of education, the philosopher-king, are all somewhat antique in their form, if indeed they could ever have been regarded as anything more than a picturesque covering for certain underlying ideas. When we ask what these underlying ideas are, we find that they are thoroughly humanistic. They are the ideas of qualitative difference and definite purpose—the

* I think they are. Writers who insist that the two statements are identical seem to forget the logical principle that a universal affirmative is not simply convertible. The statement that " all right is might " implies only that " some might is right." Still, I think it is true that the Carlylean doctrine tends to lead to the worship of force, or at least to an imperfect sympathy with those influences in human life that cannot be shown to be immediately effective.

latter being conceived as something that is to be investigated and defined by means of metaphysical speculation. For statements of a more precise and scientific kind, however, it is necessary that we should turn to Aristotle.

The first conception that we find in Aristotle is that the state is a natural and necessary element in human life, not an artificial or mechanical product. Man is φύσει πολιτικὸν ζῷον. The state is not the result of a contract, but is a natural growth from the social nature of man. The chief other point that he brings out is that, while the state was originally formed with no other end in view than the maintenance of the lives of its citizens, it is continued in existence for the sake of the development of the highest kind of life. In these conceptions we find a certain recognition of an element of truth both in naturalism and in humanism, though the emphasis is laid decidedly upon the human side. It is acknowledged that in its earlier phases the purpose which is in the end seen to be implicit in the existence of the state is not explicitly brought into consciousness ; and so in its origin the state may be said to be without clear end, or at least without that end of qualitative perfection in which its ultimate significance is to be found.

The more modern conceptions of Rousseau and

Burke are not, in their essence, very widely removed from those of Aristotle. These writers gradually substitute for the mechanical " social contract " of Hobbes the idea of a contract which is implicit in the nature of the " general will " of mankind. Now, this is what I take to be essentially involved in the humanistic conception of the political life ; and what I wish to try to bring out briefly in what follows is the way in which this may be applied to the treatment of modern politics.

One point that at once confronts us in doing this is the fact that our modern conception of the political life is so completely international as to make the precise form of earlier accounts almost entirely inapplicable. In particular, we are very far removed from that limited type of city-state which was constantly in the minds of Plato and Aristotle. But it was no doubt much more easy to regard a state of the Greek type as existing for the development of the perfect life in its citizens than it is to treat our modern cosmopolitan societies in a similar fashion. Perhaps the most hopeful case for such a purpose in our modern world would be such a nationality as Japan, with its intense unity and enthusiastic aims, based on what may be described as a social and political religion. If we are to treat European nationalities in a similar fashion, it would almost be necessary to regard them as a single unity for this purpose. And, indeed, it is almost natural for the modern sociologist to regard the whole world, or, at any rate, what we commonly call the civilized world, as the unity within which the developing life of man is to be regarded as becoming realized. If we take this point of view, the Aristotelean conception would then mean that men naturally and inevitably group themselves in a variety of social systems ; that these at first owe their origin to the simple struggle for existence, the mere effort to maintain life itself ; but that their true significance can only be discovered in the progressive unfolding of the highest characteristics of human nature. Something like this is, I believe, what we must now understand by a humanistic interpretation of the modern political life. This, it will be observed, does not involve the entire abandonment of a naturalistic interpretation of the origin of social institutions, but only the effort to see in their ultimate development the unfolding of a higher purpose. What I now wish to inquire is, how the adoption of such a point of view would affect the treatment of some of the most fundamental problems of modern politics. This question, of course, I can only hope to answer in a very sketchy fashion.

The only points to which I can here, with any hope of profit, direct your attention, are three—(1) the bearing of the humanistic point of view upon the modern conception of democracy ; (2) its bearing upon the theory of the general relations between morals and legislation ; and (3) its bearing upon international relations. Some further points, bearing more particularly upon economics and upon education, I reserve for the next two lectures.

(1) I have already indicated that the modern conception of democracy seems to me to be largely dependent on the naturalistic point of view, with which also the most flourishing period of ancient democracy tends, through the influence of Plato and Aristotle, to be associated in our minds. The belief in the absolute right of majorities, the distrust of expert opinion, the conviction that " the voice of the people is the voice of God," are thoroughly characteristic, it may be said, of that general view of the world for which quantity is supreme, while quality and inherent purpose are eliminated. On the other hand, we find that Plato, Aristotle, Burke, Comte, Hegel, Carlyle, Ruskin—almost all those whose names are specially associated with a humanistic position—may be characterized as, in one way or another, aristocratic in their tendencies. It might appear, therefore, as if humanism were

fundamentally opposed to the democratic ideal. And, in a certain sense, I think this is true. But it is partly a question of words ; and in the end I believe that the opposition here in question is illusory. The statements of Plato, for instance, have to be stripped of their poetic or pictorial wrappings before we can properly appreciate their meaning ; and then it is not so certain that they are opposed to the representative democracy of modern times. The philosopher-king, the guardians, the graduated system of education, represent undoubtedly an effort to secure the rule of the best ; but it would perhaps be too literal an interpretation to suppose that the best are to be found in certain assignable persons, or in a class clearly marked off from the others. Perhaps we should think of it, not as the rule of definite superiors, but rather as the rule of superiority in general, however it may be discovered. On the whole, it can hardly be doubted that the general influence of the Platonic conception of the state, with its great underlying conceptions of unity and brotherhood, has told quite as powerfully in support of a genuine democracy as in that of a genuine aristocracy ; and has indeed done more than almost any other single influence to enable men to realize that the two things mean the same. Aristotle, again, leans to democracy a good deal more than at first appears. It is in the πολιτέια, rather than in the kingly rule, that he seems to find in the end his really workable ideal. It should be remembered, further, that, so far as the two chief philosophers of Greece can be regarded as in essence, and not merely in name, opposed to the democratic principle, this fact is to a large extent to be connected, not with their humanism, but rather with their very imperfect grasp of the humanistic principle. What they oppose to naturalism at this point is not so much a reasoned humanism as a sort of sublimated supernaturalism. Their hankering after the philosopher-king is to a certain extent on a par with their tendency to regard the heavenly bodies as a higher form of existence than human life. For Plato human life is to a large extent regarded, not as the struggle after a realizable good, but as a falling away from an ideal perfection that is only to be found in heaven ; and, though Aristotle tries to correct this view, he is not able with any completeness to emancipate himself from it. For him also the supreme good is in the end to be thought as being realized only in a purely contemplative life, which cannot properly be regarded as human. It is this aspect of Greek thought—the aspect that leads to an opposition between the theoretical and practical life, between the ideal world and the world

of concrete process and development—rather than
its humanistic aspect, that lends support to that
aristocratic tendency, which was originally based,
after all, very largely on the traditions of a slave-
owning community, in which the industrial arts were
despised, rather than on any strictly philosophical
principle.   As soon as it is fully realized that man's
life is really to be interpreted by the purpose that
lies within it, it is at once seen that this is incompatible with the recognition of any purely external
rule.   Plato and Aristotle are really trying to bring
this out, even when they seem most emphatically
aristocratic ; but it is no doubt chiefly in such
points as this that we are led to realize that the later
ideas of Stoicism and Christianity represent a more
complete humanism than that which is to be found
in the writings of the earlier idealists.*

Their more modern counterparts may be still
more briefly dismissed.   As for Carlyle, I have already indicated that he can only be described as
humanistic with somewhat large qualifications.
His idea of the rule of the best is apt to degenerate
into a glorification of blind force, or, at any rate,
of a kind of force that is not thoroughly humane,
and that does not rest on any very subtle dis-
crimination of qualitative distinctions.   This could

* Most of the points referred to in this section are very
fully brought out in Caird's *Evolution of Theology in the Greek
Philosophers*.

hardly be said of Ruskin ; but it seems to be true, both of him and of his master, that what we find in their political teaching is a certain impatience with the cruder aspects of democratic development, rather than a carefully considered exposition of any more excellent way. On the other hand, we might refer to Rousseau, and in later times to Mazzini, as representative of a form of humanism that is thoroughly democratic ; nor should it be forgotten that the most uncompromising supporter of absolutism was Hobbes, one of the chief founders of our modern naturalistic point of view. On the whole, then, it does not appear that humanism would necessarily lead us into opposition to democracy ; but I think it is true that it must lead to some modification in the common conception of its meaning, or at least in that conception which is often most prominent in the minds both of its defenders and of its opponents. On this it may be worth while to add some explanation.

Democracy is apt to be thought of simply as a device for securing that every one's voice shall, as far as possible, have equal weight. The practice of counting votes, and the constant effort to secure that no one shall have more than one vote, tend to support this impression of its meaning. In this way it connects naturally with the utilitarian formula, that every one is to count as one, and nobody as more than one. Regarded in this way, however, democratic institutions can hardly fail to appear somewhat ridiculous to the reflective mind in their actual working. For, on the larger questions of politics, the difference between the actual number of votes on either side is seldom very great ; and, whichever party gets into power, and by however great a majority, we always find the newspapers on the other side pointing out that opinion in the country is, after all, pretty evenly divided—if, indeed, it cannot even be shown to be really in support of the losing party. At any rate, why should the opinion of 20,500 be so much better than that of 20,400 ? Schemes are, accordingly, constantly being brought forward to rectify this defect by an adequate representation of minorities ; and it is of course possible that these may do something to remove the anomaly. But the question suggests itself whether the present system of voting may not be partly interpreted and justified in another way. It might be urged that what our method of counting really means is that the 20,000 votes on each side are practically discounted ; and that it is only the marginal votes, in which the majority lies, that, properly speaking, tell at all. The underlying assumption which, on this view, justifies the procedure, is that, on contentious questions of fundamental importance, on which it is worth while to have a vote at all, it is broadly true that the worthless votes, the votes of the prejudiced and unthinking, will tend to be equally distributed on the two sides, and can consequently be eliminated, while the small majority in the margin shows the influence of thought and argument. I do not wish to press this interpretation too far ; but I believe it will be found that it is to some extent, consciously or unconsciously, a consideration that justifies, in thoughtful minds, our present methods of procedure. From this point of view the value of democracy lies, not so much in its being a means of getting at the wishes of the unthinking multitude, as in its being a means whereby the influence of thought may be made to bear on those who are susceptible of argument, and may be made a prevailing force. The true maxim of democracy, thus regarded, is not " *Vox populi, vox dei*," but " *Magna est veritas, et prevalebit*." This may perhaps suffice to indicate how democracy may be interpreted and justified from a humanistic, as well as from a naturalistic, point of view.

There is, however, still another point that is perhaps of more importance than any such considerations as these, as bringing out the bearings of humanism upon the principles of democracy.

H

It is of the essence of humanism to think of man as a being with an end. This end, moreover, is not something external to his nature, but rather something which exists for himself, and which is realized, in the main, by the unfolding of his own being. It is the growing consciousness of this, more than anything else, that has made it impossible for men to recognize any purely external rule, and that has often given to the democratic ideal a force almost amounting to that of a religion. Those who have emphasized this side may fairly be said to have been, consciously or unconsciously, speaking as humanists. Now, it is hardly possible to look at human life in this way without claiming for every one who is human that he should have some effective share in the regulation of his own life ; and in practice this almost inevitably means, among other things, that he should have some real voice in the government of his country. When, however, this point of view is adopted, it becomes at the same time clear that what is really essential is not that the voice of each should tell with equal weight, but rather that each should find a place as an organic member in the progressive life of humanity. The more fully this conception is made use of the more completely does it become possible to regard a state as a community in which, in a real sense, each may be at once sovereign and subject—sovereign in those things in which he has insight, subject in those in which he is dependent on the insight of others ; and that neither his sovereignty nor his subjection is to be regarded as involving an external rule. In this way the government becomes, not, as with Plato and Aristotle, that of a philosophic ruler, but rather that of philosophy itself ; or, to put it more correctly, that of genuine insight, whether based on science, on intuition, or on experience, and whether concentrated in one or distributed among many. The justification for the modern faith in democratic principles would seem to depend on the extent to which this kind of subordination is possible—the subordination, not of persons to persons, nor of classes to classes, but of the inferior elements in all to the superior, and of smaller ends to larger and more complete ones. Looked at in this way, democracy may be said to rest upon humanism, and to be inevitably bound up in its central principle ; but we see, I think, at the same time, that, when democracy is thus understood, it is not opposed to what Plato and Aristotle meant by aristocracy, but is rather the further development of the ends at which they were aiming.*

* For some further expansion and illustration of the points here indicated, I may refer to a paper on " The Dangers of Democracy " in the *International Journal of Ethics* for January, 1906. On the general views of Plato and Aristotle I may take this opportunity of referring to Mr. E. Barker's recent work on *The Political Thought of Plato and Aristotle.*

(2) What light, we may next ask, does the humanistic conception throw on the true relation between morals and legislation ? At first it might be thought that it tends in the direction of drawing a somewhat sharp distinction between them, and depreciating the latter in comparison with the former. A pure naturalism, it might be thought, denying the freedom of individual choice, is inclined to rest its ideal of political life on a system of compulsion, or at least of external sanctions in the form of reward and punishment ; while humanism exalts the freedom of individual choice, and tends to rest all action upon purely moral motives. And to a certain extent this antithesis is justified by facts. Hobbes, on the whole, represents such an outcome of naturalism as is here suggested ; and so perhaps do certain types of modern socialism. On the other hand, some idealistic moralists have certainly been inclined to deprecate legislative compulsion as an instrument of moral advancement, and to join in the popular cry that "you cannot make men moral by Act of Parliament." But, on the whole, it would not be easy to support this view of the contrast between naturalism and humanism in their political bearings. Indeed, on an impartial historical survey, it might seem that the antithesis is rather of the opposite character. It

is Plato and Aristotle, Hegel and Comte, Burke and
Carlyle, who make much of legislation and compulsion. It is, indeed, almost the whole point of
Aristotle's theory of politics, that the aim of legislation is to make men moral. On the other hand,
it is Mill, Spencer, and others, whose names are
associated with naturalistic views, whom we find
denouncing the " sins of legislators " in this respect,
and pleading for liberty and *laissez-faire*. Nor
ought this really to surprise us. For it is of the
essence of humanism, as we here conceive it, that
it emphasizes the growth of purpose, not in this or
that individual consciousness, but in the life of
humanity ; and, especially, if we take a view at all
akin to that of Aristotle, we must recognize this
purpose as something which does not at first fully
disclose itself, but is only gradually brought to self-
consciousness. Legislation is then naturally regarded as the instrument by which this development
is effected—in the old theological phrase, " the
schoolmaster that leads us to Christ." Thus,
humanism, while it may agree that man cannot be,
in any full sense, made moral by Act of Parliament,
may yet maintain that Acts of Parliament are an
essential phase of the moralizing process.* Natural-

* Some good remarks bearing on this will be found in Dr.
Rashdall's *Theory of Good and Evil*, Vol. I, pp. 298–9.

ism, on the other hand, tends to treat the individual either as an independent atom or as a manufactured article ; and is apt to find its ideal either in anarchism or in socialism. The ideal of humanism is found, on the whole—and this appears in nearly every writer who can really be regarded as its representative—in the form of a regulated and progressive freedom. From this point of view, however, the aim of legislation, so far as it affects the moral life of the citizen, is regarded as mainly educational ; and this is a point that I intend to emphasize somewhat further in a following lecture.*

(3) Finally, we have to ask how the humanistic conception of political life bears upon our treatment of international relations. The general point here is very similar to that which met us under the previous heading, but not quite the same. The tendency of the earlier humanists, Plato and Aristotle, to whom I have been so largely referring, was to eliminate international relations, or treat them as extraneous and necessarily hostile ; and to think of their ideal state as a self-centred community. This, of course, was natural to the Greeks, from the circumstances of their own political existence and the general stage in the course of human development at which they were ; and it must be confessed

* Lecture VI.

also that it is easier in this way to work out the conception of an ideal community, to which the individual citizens are organically related, especially if we wish to give it that sort of artistic completeness at which Plato aimed. Hence also some modern humanists, such as Fichte, have tended to think of it in a somewhat similar fashion. But it seems clear that a really humanistic conception of life in general cannot be attained in any such way as this. If the ideal life is essential to the nature of man, we cannot treat it as if it were a sort of artificial hot-house growth, cut off from the general life of the world. It would certainly be scarcely possible for any modern European nation to think of itself in this way, not merely on account of the intimate contact between the various existing nationalities, but still more on account of the way in which the lives of many nations of the past—especially the Hebrews, the Greeks, and the Romans—have become dominating factors in the thoughts, habits, and sentiments of them all. It would be equally a mistake, however, to think of a real humanism as obliterating the significance of national distinctions. The case is somewhat similar to that of the individual life. The nation cannot properly be regarded, any more than the individual, either as an independent atom or as something that may be mechanically moulded by external forces.   Here also we must recognize that there ought to be a real development helped on —perhaps even sometimes not without an element of compulsion—by the larger life of the world beyond ; while yet in the end it must be always true that all real development issues from within, and cannot ultimately be constrained.

These indications of the bearings of humanism upon the treatment of politics are no doubt rather vague and slight.   When we attempt to deal with political questions in a more detailed fashion, we soon find ourselves involved in problems that are not simply political in the narrower sense, but economical, educational, or religious ; and in the three following lectures I intend to discuss some of these ; but still my treatment of them must, I fear, continue to have a somewhat general and probably a somewhat unconvincing form.*

* The best treatment of the problems of politics from what I here describe as the humanistic point of view is that contained in Bosanquet's *Philosophical Theory of the State.*   I may also refer to MacCunn's *Ethics of Citizenship* as being of special value on certain practical questions, and to Hobhouse's *Democracy and Reaction,* in which the valuable conception of 'orthogenic evolution' is applied.

LECTURE V

HUMANISM IN ECONOMICS

IN dealing with the general subject of politics, whenever we pass from the broader questions of systems of government and international relations, and come to consider the more detailed problems by which the life of the people is affected, we at once find that the questions that confront us are economical, educational, and religious ; rather than questions of the kind that are properly reckoned political in the narrower sense of the term. We find, moreover, that these different types of problem are very intimately bound up with one another, as well as with the larger questions of government and international relations. To deal properly with any of these problems would require a larger canvass than is here provided ; but in the present lecture I intend to touch briefly on what appear to be some of the main points in connection with economics.

Among all the influences by which men's social life is affected, it cannot be doubted that economic forces are among the most powerful. Professor Marshall has expressed the view that they are more intense than any others, except those associated with religion, and that they are the most constant and pervasive. Certainly, as affecting the practical details in the life of a community, there are none that can be compared to them.

Economic forces have, moreover, a very special claim upon our attention here ; inasmuch as it is in connection with them, more than with any others, that a naturalistic theory of human society has been developed. The economic interpretation of history, such as we find in the writings of Karl Marx and others, is the most purely naturalistic interpretation. From this point of view, the explanation of all great social movements—even those that have a moral or religious character, such as changes in church organization, the prevalence or suppression of warlike preparations, changes in habits of family life, the abolition of slavery, and the like—can be traced in the end to the influence of material conditions. But, even apart from such more extreme developments of economic doctrine, it may at least be said, in a more general way, that it is in the study of economic conditions that we come most definitely upon the recognition that human life has a natural or material basis ; and this is, consequently, the aspect of sociological study that it is most difficult to humanize.

It is largely, I believe, on this account that the study of economics has tended, more than any other branch of sociology, to ally itself with the natural sciences ; and even, like most of them, to make it in some degree its ideal to subject itself to a purely mathematical method of treatment. This has, of course, been made possible chiefly through its association with that particular variety of naturalism which is dependent upon hedonism—and which, as I have already indicated, can hardly be called purely naturalistic. It was largely under the influence of Bentham and his followers that the so-called " classical " school of British economics was developed, and even in quite recent times the influence of this point of view is very clearly traceable. Even Marshall—in some respects one of the most humane of economists—has this naturalistic basis for his whole method of treatment.

Now, it is no part of my present design to criticize the applications of hedonism in economics. It is now generally recognized that it is bad psychology to say that pleasure is the only direct object of human desire, and bad ethics to say that it constitutes the ultimate good for man. But these considerations do not necessarily vitiate entirely the use that is commonly made of the conception of pleasure in economic discussions ; where, in reality, it need not be understood as meaning anything more than an object of human desire. If whatever men desire is called a pleasure, and whatever they are averse to is called a pain, the use of language may be questionable, but the results may be accurate enough to serve their purpose. The more important question remains, whether it is satisfactory to rest economic study upon the analysis of human desires and aversions ; and it is here, as I think, that what I have called the humanistic point of view affords us some light.

The essential point that here concerns us is not that an attempt is made to give a purely quantitative estimate of the forces that are operative in the economic aspect of human life. It is not here my object to deny that human life has a quantitative aspect, or that that aspect can be taken as a material for scientific study. It is no doubt true that money serves as a common measure for desires and aversions of the most varied description ; just as the amount of mechanical movement involved affords a common measure for light, heat, sound, and other physical phenomena. But there are, I think, at least two points of difference, which it is important to bear in mind.

(1) The physicist may justly contend that he has nothing to do with any aspects of the phenomena with which he is concerned other than those that are purely quantitative. The quantitative aspect supplies him with a coherent and constant material which is quite enough to form the body of a science. It can hardly be contended that this is the case in economics. The quantitative aspect varies from individual to individual, from day to day ; and, still more, from country to country, and from age to age. It was on this account that Aristotle contrasted the study of moral philosophy with that of mathematics. A young man, he urged, cannot study moral philosophy as he can mathematics ; because the material of the former is variable, and can only be apprehended through a long experience.* If this is true even of those internal aspects of conduct, with which in the main ethics is concerned, it is certainly hardly less true—in some respects even

* The critics of Aristotle have, I think, sometimes been a little unfair to him on this point. He does not mean to deny that the facts of conduct can be made objects of real scientific study, but chiefly that they cannot be simplified as purely quantitative problems can ; and that nominal definitions, such as were suggested by Socrates, are of very little value in dealing with them. It may be admitted, however, in addition to this, that Aristotle's defective psychology and imperfect view of what is meant by development, prevented him from fully realizing the extent to which problems of conduct can be brought into relation to the other facts of our experience.

more true—of those more external goods that form the subject-matter of economic study.

(2) The second point is not less important. It is that the study of economics (like the study of ethics) affects practice in a way that the study of physics does not. Light will not become any less brilliant from the fact that it is brought into comparison with sound, or that it is studied in any other way. The values of things for human thought, on the other hand, are not only variable, but they are affected, among other things, by the way in which we consider them. A thing that is treated as of no scientific importance may come in practice to lose something of its value.

On these grounds it seems impossible to give to the purely quantitative aspect of economic study the same independent position that may be given to the mathematical aspects of physics. It may be claimed that this aspect of economics has a place in the general study of the subject somewhat similar to that occupied by formal logic in the study of the search for truth. This claim, however, is certainly not a very large one ; and it may be doubtful whether even this can be fully conceded ; for it is perhaps easier to separate out the formal aspects of thought from others than it is to separate out the purely quantitative aspects in the economic side of life.

It will be observed that the points here brought forward are simply those that I have been urging all along as essential to the humanistic position. Man, on the economic side, as on other sides, must be treated differently from natural objects, because he has a history by which his intrinsic nature is affected, and because he has conscious ends. This I take to be the essential point that has been brought forward in criticism of the purely analytical method of economic study, on the part of the historical school, the ethical school, and in general those schools of thought that urge that the study of economics should be subordinated to the wider studies of sociology or social philosophy. What they all seek to emphasize is that the study of economics must be regarded as a part of the study of human life, and so as involving reference to man's qualitative ends, as well as to those aspects of life that can be treated as purely quantitative.

The importance of such considerations is more particularly apparent when an attempt is made to apply economic principles to the guidance of practical life. It then becomes evident that the purely quantitative aspects require to be supplemented by other considerations. This has, of course, been pretty fully recognized by the advocates of the analytical method of treatment. What they urge

is that the science of economics has no direct practical
bearing ; and that for guidance in practical matters
men must rely upon " common sense." A similar
view has recently been applied to the science of
ethics—notably by Mr. F. H. Bradley. In reality,
however, writers on economics and ethics are not able
to maintain such an attitude of aloofness from practical life ; and common sense continues to look to them
—and not, I think, altogether in vain—for enlightenment. Of course it is true that the detailed guidance
of the merchant, manufacturer, or leader in any industrial undertaking must in the end be left to his own
sense, assisted by that of his associates and by the
traditions of his industry and of his social environment in general ; just as the statesman, however
closely he may have studied the theory of politics,
must ultimately depend on the exercise of his own
judgment ; and just as the good citizen in general,
however much he may have exercised his mind with
speculative principles, must use in his particular
actions a certain amount of almost instinctive insight. The same is true, however, in some degree,
even of those sciences that have the most direct
bearing upon practice—even of those that are often
styled arts or practical sciences—such as navigation
or engineering. Still, it may be allowed that the
more humane a science becomes, the more directly

it is concerned with the actions of men and women, rather than with the control of natural forces, the less possible does it become to lay down general principles that can be immediately applied to particular cases. But this does not amount to saying that such sciences have no practical application. It is their business to enlighten common sense by making it clearly conscious of the most important considerations that it has to keep in mind in determining particular cases. Even Aristotle, who, more than almost any one else,* emphasized—and probably exaggerated—the variability of the conditions of human life, and the consequent inexactness of the ethical and political sciences, yet constantly treated these sciences as having a practical aim throughout. Recently, the term " normative," instead of " practical," has been commonly applied to those studies —of which logic and ethics are the most typical instances—which discuss the general guiding principles in human thought and action ; and this no doubt serves to make their real nature somewhat clearer. Now, it may certainly be maintained that the study of economics belongs, to a very large extent, to this type of science. That is to say, it is

* Others, in more recent times, who have emphasized this point, have generally connected it with some theory of development, by which the variations are to some extent explained and reduced to law.

I

one of those sciences that aim at the enlightenment of common sense in its guidance of human affairs.

Further, it would be a truly fatal error to suppose that common sense is only in need of enlightenment with regard to the instruments and conditions of action, and the tendencies of particular forces, not with regard to the general ends or ideals towards which its guidance has to be directed. What may, with more plausibility, be maintained is that different sciences are needed for these two kinds of enlightenment; and that the study of economics is concerned only with the former. But this can be maintained only so long as this study rigorously refrains from any practical application of its principles—a self-denying ordinance which it is hardly possible for any one who is really interested in his subject to carry out. As soon as we proceed to the application of principles, it becomes evident that those supplied by pure economics must be subordinated to those supplied by social philosophy. In other words, it is practically necessary to pursue the study of economics on a humanistic, as well as on a naturalistic, method.

It is, of course, not possible in such a lecture as this to bring out, with any detail, the ways in which economic study would be affected by such a method of treatment; but I may indicate three general aspects of the study on which fresh light might be expected to be thrown. These are—(1) the general theory of value, (2) the study of the conditions of economic development, (3) the control of economic forces. These points have already been emphasized by writers belonging to different schools of economic thought; the first more particularly by the ethical school, the second by the historical school, the third by the national school. To a certain extent, but not entirely, these three schools tend to be in sympathy with one another; and the same points will sometimes be found to be made by writers whose general tendencies would lead us to associate their names with different schools. It is no part of my purpose here to define these different positions; still less to discuss the doctrines of various writers who in the main adopt them. But it may be worth while to sum up what seem to me to be the chief considerations bearing upon each of the three points to which I have referred.

(1) Value, in economics, tends to mean exclusively market value; and it is usually represented as being determined by the co-operation of certain factors, especially demand and cost of production. These factors have in the end, as it is commonly supposed, a subjective foundation, demand depending on pleasure and cost of production on pain. Now,

with the qualification already indicated, I am not prepared to deny that market value may rightly enough be interpreted in this way. But value in the larger sense cannot be properly understood from this purely subjective standpoint ; and, even for purely economic purposes, it is important that this should be realized. This is a point that has been specially brought out by the ethical school of writers on economics. Ruskin, in particular, laid the foundations for such a method of treatment by his famous dictum that " the only wealth is life " — a saying that may be compared with the Socratic doctrine that " Virtue is knowledge." Just as Socrates refused to recognize goodness in actions on account of any external characteristics or on account of any traditional valuation, or of the estimation in which they are held by any individuals, and insisted that genuine insight is the only ultimate basis for goodness, so Ruskin urges * that value is not to be determined by the consideration of particular objects and their traditional uses, or by the calcula-

* What I have chiefly in mind, in suggesting this comparison, is such a statement of the Socratic position as that given in the *Phædo*—" The exchange of one fear or pleasure or pain for another fear or pleasure or pain, and of the greater for the less, as if they were coins, is not the exchange of virtue. . . . Is there not one true coin for which all things ought to exchange ?—and that is wisdom." Here Plato represents wisdom, just as Ruskin represents life, as the ultimate measure of value.

tion of the force of demand, but by the life-giving
properties of the objects that are to be valued. It
is clear that such a position might very well lead
to what Nietzsche calls an " Umwerthung aller
Werthe "—a " transvaluation of all values " ; and
this Ruskin in some degree attempted. After
laying down this general principle in *Unto This
Last*, he proceeds in *Munera Pulveris* to develop
a doctrine of intrinsic values in connection with it.
Every object, according to this view, has a definite
value which is determined by its life-producing
qualities.* I do not propose to enter further into
the consideration of this doctrine. It appears to
me to have a one-sidedness somewhat similar to
that of the doctrine of Socrates to which I have
compared it. Just as virtue is not simply insight,
so wealth is not simply life, but rather a collection
of objects found, with gradually increasing cer-
tainty, to be helpful in the realization of life. And

---

* See especially *Munera Pulveris*, chap. i, sect. 13 : " Intrinsic value is the absolute power of anything to support life.
A sheaf of wheat of given quality and weight has in it a measurable power of sustaining the substance of the body ; a cubic foot
of pure air a fixed power of sustaining its warmth ; and a cluster
of flowers of given beauty a fixed power of enlivening or animating the senses and heart." The questions that naturally
occur here are—Whose body ? Of what race ? At what age ?
Under what conditions of climate, work, and mode of life ?
Whose senses and heart ? At what level of development ?
And, Can any beauty be said to be " given " ?

just as the habits that constitute a virtuous life
are not absolutely invariable, so, but in a much
greater degree, the values of objects for the development of human life are not constant.   And just as
the general opinion of sensible people is a good,
though not an infallible, test of human virtue, so
the estimation in which objects are held is a fair,
though rough, index of their real value.   And very
often this rough index is the only one that it is
practically possible to use.   I do not, therefore,
urge that Ruskin's point of view should be absolutely substituted for the other.   But I do urge
that some attention should be given to it.

The defect of Ruskin's point of view, as I have
indicated, is that it seeks a too purely objective
estimation of values.   There is another recent view
that seems to me to contain the same defect, in a
still more exaggerated form—I mean the view that
is put forward in Mr. G. E. Moore's *Principia Ethica*.
In that book Mr. Moore deals with the conception of
good in a wide sense—a sense so wide that it seems
to me to become equivalent to that of intrinsic
value.   His contention is that good is an objective
characteristic of certain things, just as yellow is.
This view seems to me to err, still more decidedly
than that of Ruskin, in the direction of representing
value or good as having an independent existence,

without reference to its changing relations to the constantly developing life of man.

The Austrian writers, on the other hand, especially Meinong and Ehrenfels, who have sought to develop a general theory of value, extending far beyond the range of ordinary economic conceptions, appear to me to treat the matter from too subjective a point of view. Value, for them, rests ultimately on the subjective fact of valuing, not on the objective nature of the thing valued in relation to the person using it. Their conception is thus little more than an extension of the economic conception of desires and aversions, though it is more elaborately developed and covers a wider field.

Now, what I wish to urge is that humanism, in the sense in which I have been trying to explain that term, would lead us to avoid both extremes of objectivity and subjectivity. Even Protagoras, when he laid down his dictum that " Man is the measure of all things," did not, if we may trust Plato's account, apply this formula to goodness, in the same sense in which he applied it to truth. Even he recognized that one thing is better than another, in a manner that is independent of individual preference at any particular moment. This the humanist must certainly agree with, if there is to be any real meaning in his fundamental

conceptions of end and quality. On the other
hand, the humanist will tend to recognize that these
conceptions are relative to the developing life of
man, and so cannot be treated as purely objective,
absolute, or independent.*

But, it may be said, this does not at any rate
affect the treatment of market values by the pure
economist, nor would it be possible for any one,
whether economist, moralist, psychologist, or meta-
physician, to work out any definite theory of the
value of objects as thus conceived with reference to
ultimate qualities and ends. To the first of these
points I would answer that intrinsic value, in the
sense here understood, does have a pretty direct
bearing even on the consideration of market value.
Demand is being constantly affected by men's
growing insight into the things that really matter
in life ; and this is a point that cannot safely be
overlooked even by the pure economist.† With
regard to the second point, I readily allow that the

* For some further discussion of this point I may refer to
An Introduction to Social Philosophy, 2nd ed., pp. 266–71.

† Even the purest of economists will generally be found
taking some account of the real values of the objects of human
pursuit when they come to deal with such problems as those of
taxation, international trade, and the like ; but I think it is
still true to say that their general significance is not kept in view
with sufficient steadiness in many discussions of economic
principles.

treatment of intrinsic values cannot be subjected to that exact mathematical method which is applicable to the more abstract aspects of the problem of market values. The humanistic side, as I have constantly urged, is not, like the naturalistic side, purely quantitative in its character. But we should learn, I think, from Aristotle, that, though the material with which we have to deal may be inexact and variable, it is yet possible to deal with it in a way that is helpful and instructive, and even scientific. There is a constant danger of falling into the error that nothing is really scientific except what can be treated mathematically, and there could be no more fatal error from the point of view of the humane sciences, and even perhaps from the point of view of the sciences of life in general. Nothing tends more completely to divert attention from the most important aspects of the subject—those that relate to qualities and ends.

(2) This brings me to the consideration of the second way in which a humanistic point of view may be expected to affect economic study—viz. by directing special attention to the conditions of human development. The historical school has done much to bring out the importance of this aspect of the subject, and to throw light upon it ; yet the association of it with history is apt to be

somewhat misleading. A historical method of study, if by this is meant a method which interests itself in the chronicling of past facts and conditions, is not necessarily more humanistic than one that interests itself chiefly in the analysis of present tendencies. It becomes humanistic only when it is guided by the idea of human development. In short, it is not pure history, in the ordinary sense of the word, that is required for our present purpose, but rather the philosophy of history, conceived in some such spirit as that of Hegel or Comte. It may be noted that Professor Marshall, the leading representative of the purely analytical method of treatment, makes some use of this philosophical conception of history in the introduction to his *Principles ;* but I think it may fairly be said that the attempt to study the development of human life on the economic side has not as yet been carried out with a systematic thoroughness at all comparable to that which has been applied either to mathematical analysis or to the investigation of historical details. Of this we need not complain. It is a more difficult subject of inquiry, and perhaps necessarily comes after the others. My point is merely that humanism would mean, among other things, the attempt to work out this side of the inquiry more fully. And we must be content here with this general indication of its tendency.

(3) If, however, a humanistic method of study in economics tends thus to urge us back to a sympathetic study of the development of human life in the past, it is certainly no less true that it would point us forward to an attempt to understand the aims and ideals that are involved in this process of human development ; and would thus lead to a consideration of the best possible methods of guiding those economic forces whose influence the purely analytical economist seeks to study. To a certain extent such an attempt is made by all economists, even those whose tendencies are most purely analytical or most purely historical ; for practically there is no one who can entirely resist the temptation to apply his ideas to the problems of his time. But those with whose names the practical attitude is more particularly associated are probably, on the one hand, those who may be described as distinctively national—followers, in general, of Fichte or List—and, on the other hand, the various schools of socialism, who are generally international in their ultimate, if not in their immediate, aims. The national school has a special interest for us at the present time, owing to the recent revival of a somewhat similar tendency in what is commonly described as modern imperialism.

It is natural, if not almost inevitable, that those

who concentrate their attention on a social ideal of
any kind should at first think of it as a national
ideal. Even the Christian religion, now so international in its character, grew out of what was at
first an intensely national system of theocracy.
Similarly, the ideal life depicted by Plato is the life
of a self-sufficing community in the midst of a hostile
world. The more distinctively economic ideals of
modern times tend in like manner to present themselves at first as ideals that must embody themselves
in the unity of a particular state. It is only a state
that seems to be capable of supplying that systematic organization and motive force that are necessary for the realization of any large social ideal.
As I have already urged, however, it is certainly
doubtful whether a true humanism would in the
end lead us in this direction. On the economic side
we find that socialism, which began, in its more
Utopian forms, as a national ideal, tends, on the
whole, less and less—though, of course, with many
side currents—to connect itself with the state, becoming, on the one hand, local and municipal in its
efforts, and, on the other hand, international.

It seems clear, however, that the old economic
ideal of *laissez-faire* is hardly compatible with the
humanistic point of view. This ideal was based
on the strictly naturalistic conception of society as

a collection of competing elements which must be allowed to work out their destiny undisturbed ; though this view was sometimes combined with the supernaturalistic conception of an overruling providence which might be expected to elicit in the end the best possible order out of the apparently chaotic struggle. Humanism must certainly set itself in opposition to such conceptions as these ; and this is apt sometimes to be interpreted as meaning that it must lead us to the abandonment of every semblance of *laissez-faire*, and to the reintroduction of Protection and all the other forms of state control and restriction. This, I believe, to be thoroughly erroneous.

The fundamental objection to the older forms of state control rested on their arbitrary and mechanical character ; and it is hardly to be expected that the free peoples of the modern world will willingly yield themselves to any recrudescence of these. It is more and more coming to be recognized that the legitimate sphere of state control is not in the way of artificial restrictions on individual action, but mainly in the direction of education—in the widest sense of that term. The best that a state can do for its citizens—as Plato and Aristotle foresaw—is to fit them for the general work of citizenship and for the special work that they are to do as citizens.

This is primarily accomplished by the establishment of the best possible systems of general education and of the various forms of professional and technical training, but, more indirectly, by the attempt to organize the general system of life in a way that calls forth to the fullest extent the capabilities of the citizen. Of course, when the term is used in this comprehensive sense, it is not easy to draw any sharp distinction between those forms of control that are educational and those that are not ; and it may quite well be that some forms of industrial restriction could be shown to have an educational value.* All that can properly be insisted upon, from the point of view of humanism, is that such considerations should be given a paramount place in the discussion of state action. When it is fully

* This was the point that was specially emphasized by List, whose general view has been summarized as follows by Ingram : " The nation having a continuous life, its true wealth consists —and this is List's fundamental doctrine—not in the quantity of exchange values which it possesses, but in the full and many-sided development of its productive powers. Its economic education, if we may so speak, is more important than the immediate production of values, and it may be right that the present generation should sacrifice its gain and enjoyment to secure the strength and skill of the future." I mean, however, rather more than this. It is not only the " economic education " of a people that may have to be considered, but its political, moral, intellectual, and even religious education as well. But it must be admitted that it is seldom possible even for the wisest state to guide economic enterprise satisfactorily with reference to any of these forms of education.

realized, however, that it is chiefly in an educational direction that we are to look for the guidance of economic forces, it becomes clear that this need not be exclusively, or perhaps even mainly, supplied by a national government. It may be largely provided by private initiative or by international agencies.

Now I do not mean to suggest that considerations of the kind to which I here allude are not given some weight in ordinary discussions of economic questions. On the contrary, it is practically impossible to omit them in such discussions. When, for instance, a discussion is raised on such a burning question as the policy of free trade, in opposition to more or less modified forms of protection, the arguments on both sides will generally be found to be to a large extent educational in their character. The protectionist does not rest his case simply on the supposed economic benefits that would be conferred on particular industries or on particular classes of the community, but goes on to argue that certain forms of protection would tend to develop forms of industrial activity that are otherwise in danger of being checked in their growth, that others might be made instruments for the calling forth of the sentiment of national unity among related peoples, and other contentions of a similar kind. The free

trader, in like manner, does not content himself
with the general argument of economic advantage
to the world at large or to the particular nation
that is concerned, but goes on to urge the advantages of cultivating the spirit of enterprise and fore-
sight, the depressing influence of trusting to Government support, the demoralizing consequences of
a competition for favourable tariffs upon the general
political life of the community, and other similar
arguments. Now, all these arguments may fairly
be called educational, in the sense in which the
term is here understood. We cannot, then, justly
complain that such arguments are not used. What
I rather mean is that, if the study of economics
becomes increasingly analytical, or even increasingly historical, such arguments will be apt to
seem more and more to have no scientific value.
They cannot be satisfactorily tested either by
mathematical analysis or by appeal to historical
fact. And what humanism in economics would
lead us to recognize is that, notwithstanding any
such difficulty, arguments of this kind are of the
most fundamental importance ; and that an attempt
should be made to give them a real place in the
systematic discussion of economic questions. This
means, no doubt, that economic discussion must
be treated as a part of the larger discussion of

sociology and social philosophy ; and it must be fully recognized that such discussion must be expected to have that relative vagueness, inexactness, and consequent inconclusiveness that belongs to humane studies, as contrasted with those that are purely naturalistic. But my contention is that studies may be systematic, thorough, and practically enlightening even if their results are not such as can be mathematically calculated or mechanically tabulated.*

These considerations, however, carry us over very naturally to the subject of the following lecture.†

* There can be little doubt that we suffer a good deal in this country, more particularly, from the fact that our term "scientific" tends to be so much more restricted in its scope than the German "wissenschaftlich."

† Lest my references to leading modern economists should seem churlish, I may say that Professor Marshall's recent Address, published in the *Economic Journal* for March, 1907, seems to me a masterly illustration of the way in which economic questions can be humanistically treated. On the whole subject here dealt with, the articles on "Ethical Aspects of Economics" by Professor Sorley in the *International Journal of Ethics,* vol. xvii., will be found very instructive.

K

LECTURE VI

HUMANISM IN EDUCATION

THERE are two main points with which I wish to deal in this lecture—(1) the general significance of education from the point of view of humanism; (2) the special type of education that is best adapted to realize the conception that is put forward from this point of view.

The former point need not detain us long. What I have already urged in previous lectures suffices to indicate the supreme importance of education from the point of view that we are here considering. Almost all whose names are specially associated with a humanistic position, from Plato down to the most recent times, have connected their views with definite educational aims. No doubt this is true also of many—such as Robert Owen, the utilitarians, and Herbert Spencer *—who can hardly be claimed as humanists. But it is clear that human-

* Even Herbart might be said to be much more a naturalist than a humanist, in the sense in which the term is here employed. On the other hand, Carlyle, who was in the main a humanist, tended in some respects to undervalue education, and to regard

ism necessarily gives a special emphasis to education. It is hardly too much to say that the humanistic conception of the state makes education both its foundation and its crowning achievement. It looks at man as a being developing towards an end, and naturally looks to education as the means by which this development is to be effected. Naturalism, every individual as substantially bringing with him into the world all that he is ever to become. Nevertheless, the statement given above seems to me to be, in a broad sense, true. It was the element of humanism in Robert Owen—his thought of ideal men and ideal societies—that led to his interest in education ; and it was the element of naturalism in Carlyle—his view of men as somewhat blind contending forces—that led to his relative depreciation. Such exceptions are, consequently, of the kind that " proves the rule." But there is another point that it may be well to note in this connection. Naturalism is sometimes said to be equivalent to a " mechanical " view of things ; and this is true in the purely physical sense of the word ' mechanical." But, in another sense, there is nothing more human than a machine ; it is the very type of design and adaptation to an end. If, therefore, any writer has prominently before his mind some thought of an ideal aim for humanity, he is not necessarily made less humanistic by the fact that he conceives the means for the attainment of that end in a somewhat mechanical way. Bentham, for instance, so far as he was a "'psychological hedonist," might be said to have a naturalistic point of view ; but, so far as he was an " ethical hedonist," he was guiding himself by an ideal end, and had in him an element of humanism. It is the *vis a tergo* that makes the naturalist, and the idea of a good that makes the humanist ; and the two are brought together when a good is thought of as something that is to be brought about by a force that acts from behind. But I do not wish to labour this point unduly. It is not my aim to urge that a naturalist may not be enthusiastic about education, but only that a genuine humanist will almost inevitably become so.

on the other hand, in its purest forms, tends rather to accept man as he is found, and to regard education as an external instrument of efficiency, rather than as an essential element in man's life. Naturalism tends to say, for instance, that every man is to be accepted as a citizen, and allowed to have an equal voice with every other. Humanism, on the other hand, would urge that every man is, as far as possible, to be made into a citizen, or to be supplied with the necessary opportunities for becoming one; and that, as far as possible, his influence in the state should be proportionate to the use that he has made of these opportunities. Again, naturalism tends to say that the aim of social improvement is to satisfy human wants; whereas humanism tends to say rather that it is to develop human powers. In practice no doubt the results of these two ways of regarding human life may not very widely diverge, but in their essential spirit they are very far removed from one another; and this difference will generally show itself in the end in their practical results. Broadly speaking, we may say that the difference is that, from the one point of view, education is an external instrument of life, whereas, from the other, it may almost be said to be life itself. The great significance of Plato's *Republic*, I take it, which keeps it always fresh and modern, lies in its being the one great work in which this intrinsic aspect of education is whole-heartedly set forth.

This may suffice for the first point. But this naturally leads us on to inquire whether there is any special type of education to which the humanistic conception would necessarily point. And here there are some considerations that might tend at first to mislead us. The antithesis between naturalism and humanism at once suggests the corresponding antithesis between scientific studies and what are not uncommonly described as the humanities ; and there is no doubt a real correspondence here, which has some value in educational discussions ; but, unless we are careful, it may very well lead us astray. The sciences may be studied in a way that is essentially humanistic, and the humanities may be studied in a way that does not at all deserve to be so described. With regard to the humanities, in particular, there has been a considerable tendency to think of them mainly in connection with linguistic studies. History and literature are sometimes apt to be thought of as little more than subsidiary adjuncts to these ; while anything of a scientific character lies quite outside their range. So far has this been carried that, in the Scottish Universities, a Chair of Humanity means a Chair of Latin. In Oxford the

term *literæ humaniores* is used in a manner much
more nearly in accordance with what I am here
seeking to bring out, since it at least in some degree
covers philosophy, history, and literature ; but
even here the linguistic side has a certain predominance. Any one approaching Plato from the
point of view of this modern conception of the
humanities, and expecting to find him a humanist
in his educational conceptions, would be apt to be
somewhat rudely shocked. Linguistic studies would
seem to have no place at all in his educational
scheme ; the place of historical studies would appear to be extremely slight ; even literature is
hardly appreciated for its own sake ; its scope is
greatly circumscribed ; and such of it as is to be
studied is not to be read as literature, but as a means
of conveying, in a very imperfect form, true im-
pressions of what is important in human life and in
the universe in general, and of inculcating, in con-
junction with certain forms of physical training,
the right habits of the good citizen. Even this
much, moreover, is recognized only as a preliminary
and very imperfect kind of education ; and the more
excellent way which is expounded in the later books
of the *Republic* would appear to set before us a type
of education that is not at all concerned with the
humanities, but rather one that is based on mathe-

matics and that is of a thoroughly scientific character.

Yet it would certainly be a great mistake to regard Plato as an advocate of scientific education, in the sense in which such an education tends in modern times to be opposed to the study of the humanities. All the studies that he describes, whether literary, scientific, artistic or physical, are regarded from the double standpoint of furnishing a preparation for the practical life of the good citizen, on the one hand, and, on the other hand, of leading up to a true philosophical insight. So long as he can show that they subserve these purposes, Plato does not care in the least what the subject-matter is of which he avails himself, whether it be science, poetry, music, diet, gymnastic exercise, military drill, or whatever else it may be ; and, for any one who is trying to understand the value of his educational conceptions for modern times, it is probably not of much importance to consider what the subjects were to which his attention happened to be directed. This depended mainly on the actual system of education that he found at work in Greece at the time, and the directions in which knowledge happened to be developing. What he sought to do was to show how the material that he thus found at hand could be made subservient

to his special purpose.   This comes out very plainly
both in his earlier and in his later treatment of the
subject.   Literature as literature he treats almost
with contempt ; he values it only as an instrument
of a certain kind of mental and moral discipline.
And for science as science it may pretty fairly be
said that his contempt is equally great.   Astronomy,
for instance, he does not value as giving knowledge
about the actual nature and movements of the
heavenly bodies, but only as promoting reflection
and leading up to a certain general insight into the
meaning of human life in relation to the universe
in which it is placed.   It can hardly be said that
he is very successful in showing that the mathematical studies with which he deals are really fitted
to promote the kind of reflection that he has in view,
and it may even be doubted whether he was altogether serious in the attempt to show that they are
fitted for it.   Certainly it would be a great mistake
to regard him as an advocate either of a literary or
of a scientific type of education as such.   It would
be much truer to say that what he seeks to show
is that no type of education is to be valued for
what it directly is or does, but rather for the indirect way in which it can be made subservient to the
development of the highest form of human life.
It is in this sense that Plato is a humanist in educa-

tion, not in the sense that he advocates any particular kind of study as being essentially more humane than any other.

In all this, moreover, I cannot but think that Plato was wise. It is easy to exaggerate the distinction between different types of study, and to waste time in the discussion of their relative advantages. There is still some force in the homely utterance of Dr. Johnson on this subject, as to the futility of considering what should be taught first.* Moreover, it is in general true that the value of any education lies more in what it leads up to than in what it directly gives. This also, no doubt, is a point that may easily be exaggerated. It is exaggerated, I think, when undue emphasis is laid on the derivation of the word " education," and it is explained as meaning simply a development from within—an exaggeration that seems to be contained in the old Socratic method, and that is partly traceable also in the Platonic conception of education. It has to be recognized, I think, that what is important in education is not simply to bring something out from within, still less to put something in from without, but rather to bring ourselves into

* With this may be compared what is said by Dr. Rashdall, in his summing up about universities : " Up to a certain point—and this is the one consolation to the educational historian—the value of education is independent either of the intrinsic value or of the practical usefulness of what is taught."

vital relations * to all the important aspects of our surroundings, so as to use them as instruments in the development of our lives. Now, it may be taken as quite certain that all the leading aspects of our experience—science, art, literature, bodily action, etc.—can be made use of in this way ; and that no education can be regarded as complete which does not in some degree involve them all. And to a very large extent it is true that this is the lesson of Plato with regard to education ; and that it would be a mistake to look to him—or indeed to any true humanist—for any special advocacy either of science or of literature, or of any other instrument of culture, to the exclusion of the rest.

Nevertheless, it is also true that the humanistic point of view does naturally direct our attention to the special importance of what are called the humanities in education ; and does, I think, in so directing our attention, lead us to see a certain defect in the Platonic conception of education, and, still more, a certain onesidedness in some modern notions on the subject. For it does seem to be true of Plato, as I have already in some degree brought out, that he tends to think of the good that is to be

* " Vital relations " or " vital touch " is a phrase used by Principal Lloyd Morgan in this connection ; and it seems to me to express very happily the essential aim of education, as against the two opposite extremes—the mere imparting of knowledge, and the mere training of powers.

achieved through human life in a way that is not thoroughly humanistic, and that this fact tends among other things to affect somewhat injuriously his treatment of educational methods. In a more general way, Aristotle brought out this fundamental defect by saying that the good, as Plato conceives it, is not πρακτὸν καὶ κτητὸν ἀνθρώπῳ, is not something that can be done and acquired by man. It is of the nature of a far-off ideal, which must in the end be thought of as in reality independent of man and his efforts ; and this aloofness of the ultimate good colours Plato's whole way of thinking of the political life, and, among other things, his way of thinking of education. It is partly on this account that he seeks to achieve his ultimate educational end through the ministry of mathematics and the other abstract sciences. It is his distrust of human experience that sends him off on this tack, rather than his interest in the world of nature and its quantitative determinations. A thorough humanism would hardly follow him in this. It would believe that man's life is to be interpreted in the light of what it contains within itself, and would be apt to accept this as a direct object of its study.

In view of these considerations, it may not be amiss to add a little here with respect to the educational value of the humanities—a subject that is specially important at the present time. The discussion of this subject, however, tends to be not a little obscured by the vagueness in the use of the term " humanities "—a vagueness that is further enhanced by the equivalents that are sometimes substituted for it, especially in the designations of faculties and degrees, such as " Arts " and " Letters." It seems clear, from what has been already urged, that there is no absolute separation between the subjects that may be described as scientific and those that may be described as humanistic. The most extreme types are probably mathematics, on the one hand, and poetry, on the other ; but we see, from Plato's treatment in the *Republic*, that even mathematics may be regarded as having its chief educational value as a preparation for humanistic studies ; and, on the other hand, when poetry is studied mainly from the point of view of prosody or philology, it almost loses its humanistic aspect. The opposition must be regarded, therefore, not as one existing between different subjects, but rather as one between different points of view from which subjects can be regarded—though it is, of course, true that most subjects naturally tend to group themselves under one or other of these points of view. The one point of view is that of the analysis of the world as a content presented to consciousness ; the other is that of the consideration of human aims. ideals, and actions. On the one hand, we have the purely analytical sciences which tend to group themselves round mathematics, and to make use of mathematical methods ; but these branch out by degrees, and connect with the more observational sciences, in which qualitative differences play an important part ; and finally with the biological sciences, in which even aims and ideals begin to find a place. On the other hand, we have the group of subjects in which human aims and ideals are the predominant interest, such as poetry and the fine arts, literature in general, history, sociology, and the like. Philosophy may on the whole be said to be the fundamental study with reference to this group, just as mathematics may be regarded as fundamental with regard to the other ; but in both cases the fundamental study need not be directly involved in the treatment of outlying subjects in the groups. The more purely practical arts would seem to occupy a middle region between the two groups ; they involve human aims, but the interest of the studies lies mainly in the consideration of the external instruments by which these aims may be accomplished ; and thus they stand, in reality, nearer to the analytical sciences than to the humanities.

Now, from the place which these subjects occupy in the general experience and practice of mankind, it is almost self-evident that a knowledge of all of them is of great importance; and that any education is of a somewhat restricted kind which does not prepare us to regard things from both these contrasted points of view. Probably there are few, if any, who would deny this; but, from time to time, one or other side tends to be somewhat unduly emphasized, at the expense of the other side; and, in quite recent times, the value of scientific education has been made specially prominent. Hence it is perhaps profitable to indicate the value of the more humanistic studies, with special reference to the general conception of them that has here been brought forward.

The special emphasis that has recently been laid on the educational importance of the natural sciences by such writers as Herbert Spencer and others is, of course, very natural, and indeed very right. It may be traced primarily to two causes. In the first place, it is part of the general reaction against purely classical studies. These, as I have already indicated, have tended to be pressed forward as the exclusive representatives of humanistic studies; and, of course, there are many historical reasons that explain, and to some extent justify, the predominance that has been given to these studies. Into these we need not here enter.

It is enough to say that many educationalists have come to feel that this predominant position can no longer be fully justified ; and the natural sciences form, on the whole, the most compact group of studies that can be offered in their place. In the second place, a more positive ground for the advocacy of the study of the natural sciences readily presents itself in the supreme interest in the views of the world that these sciences have recently disclosed, and in their increasing importance as the foundation for the practical arts of life, and indeed even for the fine arts themselves.

Now, I am far from wishing, even in the slightest degree, to disparage scientific studies. What I wish to urge is only that an equally good case can be made out for the study of the humanities when the nature of that study is properly conceived. In order to bring this out, I will call your attention to some of the chief points that can be urged in support of scientific studies, and endeavour to show that arguments of a similar kind can easily be urged in favour of the humanities. In doing this I, of course, make no pretence to exhaustiveness in the considerations that are brought forward.

(1) Undoubtedly one of the strongest claims that scientific education can make upon our attention lies in the intrinsic greatness of its theme. The

sciences seem to form a connected body of doctrine, opening up to us the means of gaining insight into the whole structure of the material universe, and even promising to throw much light upon the development of human life and thought. To enter this realm is to become a freeman of the kingdom of knowledge ; to remain out of it is to be for ever incapable of appreciating those great ideas that have for the instructed transformed the whole conception of the universe, and that even for the uninstructed have almost changed the aspect of the world. This view of science gives it a hold on the imagination, and makes it, when skilfully handled, an inspiring instrument of education. In contrast with such transcendent claims, the humanities may well seem tame and unattractive, especially when they are conceived as mainly linguistic. In such studies we seem to be dealing merely with the efforts that men have made to express their ideas, rather than with the great ideas themselves ; and, even if some study of human history is added, this may well appear to be in large part a chronicle of failures and follies.

There is, however, another side to all this. The study of human life, when properly conceived, is certainly as large and as inspiring a subject as the study of the material universe. If it does not appear so, the fault must lie rather in the way in which it is presented than in its own intrinsic nature. Indeed, if we set aside its reference to human life, the study of the material world loses both its interpretation and its use. Apart from this, it becomes little more than a calculation of magnitudes and motions. The study of human life, on the other hand, does not mean merely the examination of the words by which ideas are conveyed, nor the record of dynasties, wars, or commerce. It means the acquisition of insight into the great qualities of human nature and the actions that grow out of them. It means the study of the meaning of citizenship, the appreciation of fortitude, sympathy, insight, beauty, moral and religious aspiration ; and these things, after all, are greater than anything that we know of the stars or of the atoms.

(2) Apart from the greatness of its theme, scientific education claims attention on account of the objective reality of its subject-matter. It deals, as it is often said, with things instead of words. Here again we are brought back to the great objection against humanistic studies, that they are apt to be predominantly linguistic. In spite of Browning's *Grammarian's Funeral*, few are prepared to see much sublimity in the determination " not to

L

live but know "—at least when the matter to be known is mainly philological ; and it is, at any rate, forcibly urged that most men must aim at living, and that education in general should be a preparation for life. From this point of view, studies of a purely linguistic kind are apt to seem mere pedantry—the essence of which, as I suppose, lies in mistaking the instruments of education for education itself. Now, I do not think it can be denied that there is some truth in this. The astronomer is not likely to substitute an interest in telescopes for an interest in the stars ; and probably it is in general true that the scientific student has his attention more constantly directed to the real objects of interest than the student of more humane subjects. Man, as Carlyle was so fond of reminding us, wears clothes and uses tools ; and, in studying man, we constantly find ourselves looking at the clothes and the tools, instead of at human life itself. In answer to all this, however, it may be urged that this antithesis is to some extent superficial. If it is the essence of human life to pursue conscious ends, this involves the adaptation of conscious means to these ends ; and this, I suppose, is what is meant by defining man as a " tool-using animal." If so, the study of these tools can hardly be altogether irrelevant ; and certainly words are among the most remarkable and essential of all tools for the development of human life. It might even be urged that words are more than tools. They are a natural growth, and stand constantly in the most vital relation to man's development as a thinking being. They may in this way even be compared to the facts of external nature, which also may be regarded (as Berkeley urged) as a kind of language, an expression of under-lying principles. In this spirit it has been said that

> " Words, like Nature, half reveal
> And half conceal the soul within."

Words, in short, *are* things, and indeed very living things. The complete answer to the charge here made against humanistic studies is to be found, however, in the more thorough recognition that linguistic studies are only a part, and not the most fundamental part, of what ought to be understood by the humanities. Modern educationalists are beginning to recognize that it may not even be necessary to begin with the study of words in the teaching of children.

(3) This leads us, however, to another point in which some educational advantage may be claimed for the natural sciences—especially those of an observational and experimental character. However real the facts of human life may be, it may be

urged that they are at least in general somewhat beyond the observation and experience of the young. The objects of nature, it may be said, are more immediately apparent to the senses, and can thus be utilized for educational purposes at an earlier stage. The essential facts of human life, on the other hand, can only be spiritually discerned. They depend on the development of emotion and imagination and even of a kind of introspective analysis which is foreign to the nature of young children. This is, I think, to a large extent true ; and it forms a valid ground for the introduction of what is called " nature-study " at an early stage in education. But it would be easy to exaggerate the importance of the point here made. Chairs and houses and other objects of human contrivance can be observed as readily as most natural products ; and an interest in the habits and aims of those who make and use them can pretty soon be developed. As for the higher faculties of feeling, imagination, and reflection, it must, no doubt, be left to those who have made a special study of the development of children to determine the stage and the manner in which these can best be cultivated ; but it seems clear, at any rate, that it would be a fatal mistake to let these higher capacities be stunted in order to bring out the power of observation. The very fact that they are more difficult and complex, and less natural to the young, makes it all the more important to watch for opportunities of introducing them. It is noteworthy, as I indicated before, that Plato's advocacy of scientific study is based on quite the opposite ground—viz. that such study leads us to distrust our senses, and so promotes reflection. But this has reference to the mathematical sciences ; and it is very doubtful whether Plato made out his point. On the whole it is probably true that the observational sciences should somewhat precede the more humane studies in a complete educational course. Rambles in the woods may naturally come before rambles in history and literature ; but it remains true that the humanities provide educational elements that cannot be found in the natural sciences ; and that it is important to give attention to the development of this side at as early a stage as is possible.

(4) The advantage that has just been claimed relates mainly to the observational sciences. But in recent years the claims of the more definitely experimental sciences have been perhaps even more enthusiastically urged. For these it is especially claimed that, in connection with them, children can be taught, not merely to observe things directly for themselves, but also to do something and make

fresh discoveries. Now, this is a point that it
specially behoves us here to notice ; for it may
fairly be said that it is an essentially humanistic
point. Man is a doer as well as a seer ; and it is
part of the special mission of humanism to emphasize man's aims in action. Now, it may be
maintained, that though this point is humanistic,
yet the natural sciences provide more scope for the
development of this side of our nature than what
are called the humanities. It is impossible, it may
be urged, to experiment with human life as we can
with natural objects. The kind of action that can
be cultivated in connection with the humanities, it
may be said, is necessarily very limited. It takes
the form mainly of literary composition, and possibly
artistic production ; and even this must necessarily
be rather slight and imitative. This point also
seems to me to be a real one ; though here also
it is easy to exaggerate the difference. After all,
the experiments of the young in science can hardly
be very freely initiated. It is probable that, for
those who have any natural talent, literary and
artistic production is more likely to stimulate
originality. But, what is much more important,
it is apt to be overlooked that there is a much more
extensive side of action which naturally connects
with the humanities—viz. all that comes under the

head of moral conduct. It is not possible to discuss here the best methods of conveying moral instruction ; but I believe it will be generally allowed that it must be introduced, very largely, in connection with the literature and history of the human race. It will generally be allowed also that it should be introduced in such a way as not merely to be an object of intellectual interest, but something which at once becomes effective in action. If this side of education were more systematically developed it would, I believe, very largely supply anything that may be lacking on the more practical side of the humanities.

(5) So much for the advantages of the observational and experimental sciences. There is, however, another educational advantage that may be claimed for both these groups, and that belongs still more emphatically to sciences of a mathematical character, viz. the exactness of the knowledge which they convey. Knowledge of a similar kind is hardly to be found in the humanities. A large part of history must always be conjectural ; and the significance of the greater part of literature has to be felt rather than explicitly stated. When exactness is sought in such subjects, it can generally only be reached by pedantry and peddling details. Literature is thus in danger of being swamped by philo-

logy, and history by chronology. I think it must be allowed that this is a real danger in the teaching of the humanities. What is best in them is an evanescent essence, which loses its value when it is bottled up and labelled. This is a difficulty that cannot be evaded, but that may in large measure be removed if it is boldly faced. What it points to is the need of securing the right kind of teachers for subjects of this sort. This being recognized, it is surely an advantage in education that not all subjects should be capable of being dealt with in a mechanical fashion, that there are some that demand the higher qualities of mind and spirit. The exactness of the natural sciences means, in the main, as we have seen, that they tend to be purely quantitative. The best things in life have to be estimated in quite another way ; and any type of education would be gravely defective which should habituate the mind to the idea that measurable magnitudes are all-important.*

* Sir William Hamilton's essay on " The Study of Mathematics " is, of course, monstrously one-sided ; but one of his points (which, after his manner, he enforces by a bewildering " cloud of witnesses ") appears to be a sound one—viz. that mathematical studies accustom the mind too much to purely deductive reasoning, and tend, if too exclusively followed, to incapacitate it, in some degree, for the estimation of probabilities and the apprehension of ultimate principles. The extent to which philosophy, in particular, has suffered, both in ancient and in modern times, by the application of mathematical methods, is

(6) Another educational advantage that may be claimed for the natural sciences is to be found in the fact that they form, more obviously than the humanities, a connected and systematic unity. Plato was able to bring this out even with reference to the sciences as they existed in his time, and to represent them as a regular scale leading up from arithmetic to dialectic ; but, of course, the modern doctrine of the correlation of the physical forces, combined with the general theory of evolution, has made the unity of the sciences still more apparent. In contrast with these, the humanities are apt to present the appearance of a somewhat chaotic mass of materials, fragments of history, language, literature, morals, economics, with no definite beginning, middle, or end. This is, however, a disadvantage that is clearly in process of removal. It has come to be seen, for instance, that languages are not so distinct from each other as they once appeared, and that many of them can almost be

altogether incalculable. From the Pythagoreans to Descartes and Spinoza, and from these (as I think) to Royce and Russell, they have proved the most fertile source of plausible and seductive fallacies. In economics and in pure logic mathematical methods are perhaps more in place ; but even there I am afraid they often tend to withdraw the mind from concrete considerations, which are in reality more important. Exactness is certainly desirable ; but it is a fatal error to secure it by leaving out the main content, or the qualifying conditions.

treated as if they were dialects of one language. History also is ceasing to be a chronicle of events that took place in this, that, and the other country ; and it is becoming more possible to regard it as the record of the development of man's social life. Literature is, in like manner, coming to be seen as a developing whole ; and philosophy, especially through the influence of the Hegelian conception, is coming to be treated, not as the opinions of a variety of writers, but as the human mind trying to grasp the universe. It will perhaps always be true that the natural sciences will form a more compact body of knowledge than the humanities, and that their connections will be more easily defined ; but we may reasonably hope, at any rate, that the humanities also will soon be recognized as a unity, the systematic account of the gradual unfolding and expression of the spirit of man.

(7) It may be doubted, however, whether any of the advantages to which I have referred have weighed so much in popular estimation as the more purely utilitarian value of the natural sciences. The natural sciences are recognized as the foundations of those practical arts on which so much of our modern civilization depends ; and it is as the basis of these practical arts that they are chiefly valued by many of their recent supporters. Now, I have

no desire here to disparage these applications, or the kind of civilization that rests upon them ; nor indeed do I wish to deny that, in a sense, education ought to be utilitarian—i.e. that it ought to be a preparation for the achievement of the great ends of life, whatever these may be. But there are two points that I wish to urge. The first is, that we may easily make the mistake of looking out for too immediate uses in education. It is recognized, I believe, by the most enlightened advocates of technical education, that it is of comparatively little real value unless it rests on a basis of sound theoretical knowledge. It is but a step from this to see that specialized theoretical knowledge is of little value unless it is guided by good general intelligence and wide interests. If so, the development of these must be the most important matter, even from the point of view of practical utility. The second point that I wish to make is that the humanities are by no means so far removed from practical use as is sometimes imagined. This is a point that I have already to some extent brought out in dealing with another aspect of the subject. In arranging early forms of education, in particular, it is evidently impossible to provide a very specialized preparation for life, even if it were desirable to do so. We are not all preparing to be engineers or doctors ; and very often we cannot at first foresee, with any definiteness, what we are preparing to become. The one thing that we do know is that we are all preparing to be men or women. For this purpose some study of human life can hardly be irrelevant. What is above all things needed is that we should from the first acquire a truly humane attitude and outlook. This is, I suppose, what is meant by those who maintain that all education is moral, that its great object is the formation of character— statements that are often little better, it is to be feared, than cant phrases. Now, it would evidently be beyond the scope of such a lecture as this, or even of such a course of lectures as this, to consider the precise place of moral and religious instruction in a scheme of education. It is enough for my purpose to urge that these—including in them, of course, the study of what is meant by citizenship—must be in the end the most practical and useful elements in education, lying at the basis of all the rest ; and that they obviously connect more directly with the humanities than with the natural sciences.

I hope I have made it sufficiently apparent that it has not been my object to advocate any particular type of education, as against all others. In education, as in most other practical affairs, we must learn wisdom, in the main, by the trial of different methods ; and I certainly cannot lay claim to any experience that would justify me in pronouncing upon the superiority of any one, even if I thought it at all likely that any one is, in all respects, preferable to all others.   My aim has merely been to show the significance of the humanistic point of view as bringing out the place and value of certain educational elements.   In reality, I conceive that the two great instruments of education to which I have been referring—the humanities and the natural sciences—must be brought together into very close connection in any educational system that aims at completeness ; and, in particular, I think that they necessarily come very closely together as soon as we try to make education bear upon any of the larger interests of life—especially as soon as we try to make it an instrument of moral and religious training. On this I have only been able to touch very slightly in this lecture.   It is a very large and thorny question ; and it could not, in any case, be properly handled until we have, to some extent, considered the subject of the next lecture—the general bearing of humanism on religion.*

* In connection with the points dealt with in this Lecture, reference may be made to Fouillée's *Education from a National Standpoint*, to H. M. Thompson's *Essays in Revolt*, and to the *Essays on a Liberal Education*, edited by Farrar (published in 1867, but still worth reading).

LECTURE VII

HUMANISM IN RELIGION

IN the last three lectures I have tried to give various illustrations of the ways in which the fundamental conceptions of humanism can be applied in different departments of life. In doing this I have not sought to advocate the humanistic point of view as the only valid way of throwing light on the great problems that emerge in these different departments. I have brought it forward as one way of looking at life, a way that may serve to supplement others, and that may in some respects carry us deeper than others, rather than as a way that is absolutely ultimate and complete in itself.

The speculative question of the sufficiency of humanism as a philosophical standpoint has, consequently, not come into prominence. When we pass, however, to the consideration of the place of religion in life, we are almost inevitably brought back to that more fundamental problem. For a religious point of view seems necessarily to set itself up as complete and ultimate. It is not content to be regarded as simply one way among others in which things may be regarded. If it is to be accepted at all, it must be accepted as the deepest and most absolute truth about the universe. It may be well, therefore, to remind ourselves again at this point of the meaning that we have attached to humanism, and of the place that it occupies among other theoretical positions.

I have used the term throughout as the antithesis of naturalism, as expressing the point of view that tries to interpret man in his own light, and the universe in the light of man ; whereas naturalism seeks rather to interpret the material universe in its own light, and man in the light of the material universe.

I have, however, recognized that, while these two positions may be regarded as antithetic, there is a third that is, on the whole, opposed to both, viz. the position of supernaturalism, which seeks the explanation of the universe, or of its most important aspects, in something that transcends both nature and human life. Now, religion is generally supposed to rest on some form of supernaturalism. At its highest levels, at any rate, it seems to involve something of the kind that Wordsworth describes as

> " A sense sublime
> Of something far more deeply interfused,
> Whose dwelling is the light of setting suns,
> And the round ocean and the living air,
> And the blue sky, and in the mind of man ;
> A motion and a spirit, that impels
> All thinking things, all objects of all thought,
> And rolls through all things." *

And even when its object takes a form less vast and elevated than this, it seems at least to carry us far away from the objects that are immediately before us in our ordinary experience, whether in our own lives or in the world around us, and beyond the principles by which these are commonly interpreted, and to present us with what is in some degree mysterious and transcendent. Yet it may pretty safely be said that no religion is entirely of this character. They all, in some way or other, make their appeal in the end to the human senses and the human heart, however far they may seek to raise us beyond what is directly contained in these. Indeed, it seems clear that the opposition between supernaturalism, naturalism, and humanism cannot be accepted as an absolute one. There is practically no pure supernaturalism ; no religion and no in-

---

* It is perhaps worth noting here that Wordsworth character-izes this ultimate object of reverence as " a motion and a spirit," thereby ascribing to it the fundamental determinations both of the naturalistic and of the humanistic conception of reality.

telligible speculative position leaves us in the end face to face with mere mystery, with something that cannot be brought into any real relation to our inner and outer experience. On the other hand, naturalism and humanism seldom profess to be absolutely complete in themselves. Naturalism usually ends in agnosticism, and so brings us back to the region of mystery ; and what begins as humanism generally leads us to some conception of a personality that transcends all ordinary experience. If it is true that all religion has a trace of supernaturalism, it seems also to be true that no religion is simply supernatural ; but rather that every religion leans either towards naturalism or towards humanism. We may, consequently, at this point also, continue to recognize these two main positions as dominating human thought.

The general antithesis between these two positions, as it affects religion, has perhaps never been more strikingly brought out than in Kant's famous account of the two great objects of human reverence. " Two things fill the mind with ever new and increasing admiration and awe, the oftener and the more steadily we reflect on them : *the starry heavens above and the moral law within.* I have not to search for them and conjecture them as though they were veiled in darkness or were in

M

the transcendent region beyond my horizon ; I
see them before me and connect them directly with
the consciousness of my existence. The former
begins from the place I occupy in the external world
of sense, and enlarges my connection therein to an
unbounded extent with worlds upon worlds and
systems of systems, and moreover into limitless
times of their periodic motion, its beginning and
continuance. The second begins from my in-
visible self, my personality, and exhibits me in a
world which has true infinity, but which is traceable
only by the understanding, and with which I discern
that I am not in a merely contingent, but in a universal and necessary connection, as I am also thereby
with all those visible worlds. The former view of a
countless multitude of worlds annihilates, as it were,
my importance as an *animal creature*, which, after
it has been for a short time provided with vital
power, one knows not how, must again give back
the matter of which it was formed to the planet it
inhabits (a mere speck in the universe). The second,
on the contrary, infinitely elevates my worth as an
intelligence by my personality, in which the moral
law reveals to me a life independent on animality,
and even on the whole sensible world, at least so
far as may be inferred from the destination assigned
to my existence by this law, a destination not re-

stricted to conditions and limits of this life, but reaching into the infinite."* Here we have a very distinct statement of the contrast between man regarded from the naturalistic point of view and man regarded from the humanistic point of view, and the recognition that from each point of view a certain ultimate object of reverence presents itself. On the one hand we have the boundless extent of natural forces, in comparison with which the religious consciousness exclaims, " What is man that thou art mindful of him ! " On the other hand we have the thought of duty or goodness, which we find only in human life, and which seems to give us a qualitative superiority over everything else that we know. Power and goodness, natural force and human force, these, it may be said, are the great objects of our veneration ; just as it is the lack of either of them that fills us with our deepest despair.

"The good lack power, but to shed idle tears ;
The powerful goodness lack—worse need for them."

This is Shelley's despairing utterance ; and it may be said at once that no religion would seem to be really fitted to fill the wants of the human heart unless it is able to bring these two sides together. But religions that lean to one side or the other may partly serve their purpose.

* Conclusion of the *Critique of Practical Reason* (Abbott's translation).

Pure naturalism, indeed, can hardly serve as a basis for any religion. We can hardly worship purely physical forces, such as light, heat, or electricity, or material bodies, such as the sun, moon, and stars, so long as they are regarded simply as physical forces or as material bodies. It was not the sun that the Greeks worshipped, but the bright god Apollo, driving in his glorious car and shooting his irresistible arrows. The light that is worshipped by the Persians is not merely, or mainly, the light that is analysed through the prism, but rather the light that shines chiefly in the soul of man. Still, it is undoubtedly possible to take naturalism as the basis for a sort of religion; and this has often enough been done by scientific thinkers, though probably it has not often had much hold on the popular imagination or much influence on the larger movements of human life and action. The religion of the Stoics might to some extent be regarded as belonging to this type; though its naturalism is very largely qualified by the fact that the nature of which they speak is also thought of as reason and as a source of moral obligation. The geometrical God of Spinoza—*deus sive natura*—might also be taken as an illustration of a similar tendency; and indeed his general position very closely resembles that of the Stoics. But here again we have to remember that the God of Spinoza is thought as well as extension. Though it is, in Hegel's phrase, substance instead of subject ; yet it is at least supposed to be, among other things, a thinking substance. Mr. Bradley's conception of the Absolute is another instance that naturally occurs ; for though this is said to be spiritual and individual, yet it seems to be emptied of most of the specific content that constitutes man as we know him. Yet this can hardly be described as a naturalism ; it is rather a sort of supernaturalism, in which nature and man are absorbed. And indeed the same is true even of the unknowable God of Herbert Spencer, which is said to be super-personal, and which forms the foundation for the most philosophical type of that kind of religion that is known as agnosticism. Apart from these more or less philosophical conceptions, none of which is really, in any full sense, naturalistic, it would be difficult to point to any religion that rests to any large extent on naturalism ; though, of course, it is easy to point to many in which the forces of nature play a prominent part. We may add, I think, that, so far as religions are naturalistic, their interest for sociology at any rate is, in the main, negative ; it is not such religions that serve, to any considerable extent, as animating forces in the social development of man.

When we pass from these to the more humanistic
types of religion, we are apt at first to suppose that
humanism means the same thing as anthropomorphism ; and this may easily set us off upon a
wrong scent. We are led in this way to think of
the " fair humanities " of the Greek religion as the
supreme example of this type of worship. Nor
indeed do I deny that it may to a large extent be so
regarded. But we must not forget the penetrating
comment of Hegel, that the great defect of the
Greek religion was that it was " not anthropomorphic enough." This, I take it, does not merely
mean that their representation of human life is
incomplete—that their picture of humanity is too
beautiful and triumphant, and that they do not
sufficiently, like another great religion, present us
with " a man of sorrows " (though they do present
us with a man of labours). It means rather that
the Greek point of view, though in the ordinary sense
anthropomorphic, is not really humanistic, in the
sense in which that term is here employed. Man is
depicted rather in his external aspect than in the
inner significance of his life, and so rather as a part
of nature than as distinctively human. And in
fact, when we inquire further, we soon find that most
of the Greek divinities stand primarily for the great
powers of nature rather than for human person-

alities or human ideals. Hence the gods have to be supplemented by the heroes ; and it is rather in Heracles than in Zeus that we find the dawning of a genuine humanism. Similarly, when Carlyle, following out his idea that religion is essentially hero-worship, points us to the Scandinavian divinities as an illustration, he seems to be, in the main, leading us astray.* These also represent primarily the rude forces of nature much more than human efforts or ideals ; though it is true that nature is to some extent depicted on the analogy of the life of man.

Anthropomorphism, in short, in the sense of the tendency to represent the object of worship in a definitely human shape, is by no means the best test of humanism in religion. What is essential is rather a reverence for those qualities that are deepest in man's nature, and especially his recognition of a moral end. In this sense, such a religion as Buddhism, which makes very little appeal to the external features of man's life, is more truly humanistic than the religion of the Greeks. Now, I believe it will be found that the humanistic tendency in religion, understood in this sense, is a constantly growing one, and is to be found most strongly

* It seems to be true, however, that, in the worship of Odin we see the gradual emergence of a humanistic conception out of the more primeval naturalism.

marked in those religions that have taken the greatest hold on men's lives, and that have been the sources of the most far-reaching movements in history. Primitive man tends to take as his objects of reverence those things that appeal most forcibly to his senses, and that seem to limit and control his actions. These he, no doubt, tends to picture to himself as living powers, acting on principles similar to those of which he is more or less conscious in himself. It is these tendencies that give rise, at their highest point, to such elaborate mythologies as those of Scandinavia and Greece. The more reflective consciousness, on the other hand, which has become more profoundly conscious of what is of the highest importance in its own life, turns away from these external representations, and is not prepared to accept anything as an ultimate object of worship, except that which embodies its own ideals. Now, it is of course not possible for me here to make any attempt to trace the forms in which these tendencies show themselves in the great historical religions of the world,* but I think it may serve to bring out the main points that I have in view if I call attention briefly to the growth of humanistic influences in some of those modern forms of religious thought

* This has been, to a large extent, done in Caird's masterly book *The Evolution of Religion.*

with which we may be supposed to be most familiar.
In doing so it will be necessary for me to indicate
the views that I have formed on various movements
in a way that may be more dogmatic, and less
qualified, than I could wish. This is inevitable in
a short sketch, such as the present.

The religion of the Jews, on which that of modern
Europe is so largely dependent, was certainly, in
the sense here understood, an eminently humanistic
religion. It is clear, whatever we may think of it
otherwise, that it is specially characterized by the
spirituality of its conception of the divine nature,
and by the strenuous efforts that were made by its
adherents to avoid mixing up the apprehension of
this purely spiritual being with any kind of material
representation. Of course we know that it was
found very difficult to sustain the purity of this
conception, and we may readily trace successive
stages in the working of it out. We learn also, and
surely not with any great surprise, that the people
showed a constant tendency to relapse into those
more naturalistic forms of worship that were
common among the people around them. The
representation of the divine being as a sort of
national leader, the Lord of Hosts, strong in battle,
is, no doubt, hardly compatible with the deeper
conception of God as being, in the famous phrase

of Matthew Arnold, " a power, not ourselves, that makes for righteousness." \ The form of worship also, the sacrifices and other rites, bear undeniable traces of the practices that belong to more natural-istic types of religion ; and it is only among the latest exponents of the creed that we find these definitely decried, and the explicit recognition sub-stituted, that purity of heart and nobility of life are the only sacrifices that are really acceptable—the sacrifice of the baser side of our nature on the altar of the higher.　But it seems sufficiently clear that it was in this truly humanistic direction that the Hebrew type of religion was developing throughout.

Christianity again, as I conceive it, is best under-stood as a carrying farther of this spiritualizing tendency.　The national aspect is completely set aside.　What we are concerned with is no longer the religion of the Jews, but a religion that lays claim to the homage of the world.　And, with this widening of its basis, its aggressive attitude neces-sarily disappears.　The divine being is no longer the Lord of Hosts, conquering Canaan and driving out the heathen, but rather a being of universal love, the friend of the meek, who are to inherit the earth.　With this change also, we are led away from the conception of the divine being as a stern law-giver, thundering commandments from Sinai.　Love

is substituted for law ; and the divine voice is found
rather in our own consciousness than in any external
authority. All this certainly constitutes an immense step in the direction of humanism. Its significance is well summed up in Browning's " Epistle
from Karshish "—

> "So, the All-Great were the All-Loving too:
> So, through the thunder comes a human voice
> Saying, 'O heart I made, a heart beats here!
> Face, my hands fashioned, see it in myself!'"

This is, in the deepest sense, anthropomorphic.
God is conceived as in the image of man, man as
the most complete expression of the divine nature.
With this comes the idea of the infinite and exclusive worth of the individual life. "What shall it
profit a man if he gain the whole world, and lose his
own soul ? " Again, as with Browning, it is the
history of a soul that alone matters. The conception of immortality naturally goes with this—
immortality conceived, not, as with Plato, as the
immortality of thought, or the persistence of a certain
inner essence, but rather as a personal and individual
survival. So far, then, we seem to have in Christianity a completed humanism. Further consideration, however, seems to show that, in its first
presentment, there is a certain vagueness, if not
even a certain contradiction. If the divine is
identified with the human, the identification is yet

not direct and immediate. If the kingdom of heaven is within us, it is yet a kingdom that can only be gained by a terrible struggle. If, in one sense, " I and My Father are one," yet it remains very emphatically true also that " My Father is greater than I." Here we seem to have the antithesis between the microcosm, with its ideal struggling for realization, and the macrocosm, in which that ideal is to be conceived as completely achieved. If goodness is the inner essence both of man and of God, in man at least it has not the perfect power of working itself out. Hence there is a separation, after all, between the divine and the human, and a need of atonement. This leads, in certain types of Christianity, to a separation between the divine and the human, which may be said even to become more intense than in most other forms of religion. Sometimes it even becomes an " other-worldliness," an effort after a good to be achieved by the individual in a future mode of existence quite distinct from this. Yet, at any rate, the conviction is never wholly lost that the good for man is the supreme good.

It is, of course, quite beyond our scope to make any attempt to trace the way in which this Christian conception has worked itself out. I can only refer, in the briefest possible way, to some fundamental points that seem to illustrate what I am specially seeking to emphasize. In the conception of the Holy Ghost, for instance, and in the growth of Roman Catholicism, I think we may see, in some respects, a further humanizing of the Christian conception. The divine is made more thoroughly human by being expressed, not merely in a single personality long since removed from visible life, but in a persistent organization spreading over the civilized world, and in which there is contained, in a high degree, power as well as goodness. The worship of saints, and especially of the Virgin Mother, adds a further humanizing touch, though it tends also, to some extent, to lead us back to anthropomorphism in the lower sense. But, with all qualifications, the establishment of the conception of a kingdom of heaven upon earth, preparing the way for a more complete realization afterwards, was surely a great step in the development of a truly humanistic religion.

Protestantism, on the other hand, may seem at first to lose a great part of the humanism that is contained in Catholicism ; and, in some of its forms at any rate, this may really be the case. But on the whole, it may be regarded, on the one hand, as an effort to clear Catholicism of that lower element of anthropomorphism into which it tended to relapse, and, on the other hand, to protest against the externalization of religious authority. There are, of course, many different types of Protestantism; and it is difficult to say much that is true as a characterization of them all. But in general it may be said to be opposed to the external power of priestcraft, and to insist rather on bringing the individual consciousness into a more direct and intimate relation to the divine.* Its aim and significance are largely summed up in the lines of Tennyson—

> " Speak to Him, thou, for He hears, and spirit with spirit
>   may meet :
> Closer is He than breathing, and nearer than hands and
>   feet."

* It has been urged, in opposition to this, that the essential point of Protestantism lay, not in its insistence on the right and duty of private judgment, and the consequent directness of relation between the divine and human, but rather on the substitution of the authority of the Bible for that of the Church. This is to some extent true ; but not, I think, as true as is often supposed. In any case, the authority of a book, or collection of books, even if regarded as absolute and infallible (and few Protestants would maintain so much), must, in any case, be very different in kind from the authority of a living and active organization. And, indeed, we all know what the authority of the Bible, without any authoritative interpreter, comes in practice to mean.
 " Hic liber est in quo quærit sua dogmata quisque ;
    Invenit et pariter dogmata quisque sua."
To send people to try to interpret for themselves the literature of the Jews must mean, to a very large extent, to throw them back upon their own spiritual discernment, with such guidance as they may chance to find. The Church of England, of course, in this as in other respects, has sought (perhaps wisely) to discover a *via media* between the Roman Catholic and the more strictly Protestant attitude ; and this is in some degree true of other religious communities as well. But, on the whole, the characterization of the Protestant attitude that is given in the text above seems to me to be substantially accurate.

This gives us a pure humanism, freed from anthropomorphism. At the same time, it tends to bring into clearer relief the difficulty of Christianity which Catholicism had on the whole evaded and concealed —the difficulty, namely, that the unity of the divine and human is rather an aspiration than a reality, something that was done and may be done, rather than something that is done here and now. In face of this difficulty, some forms of Protestantism have even appeared to relapse into something closely akin to the older religion of the Jews, separating the divine once more from the human, and representing it as an external authority above us. On the other hand, some of the more recent tendencies in religious thought appear to be rather more in sympathy with Catholicism than with Potestantism, largely from a consciousness of this great inherent danger. This may be said, for instance, to be true, in different ways, of religious teachers so far removed from one another in most other respects as Carlyle and Comte.

Carlyle and his disciple Ruskin represent a certain distrust of the independence and individualism of extreme Protestantism, and seek for a reorganization of society in some respects akin to that attempted and partially achieved by Catholicism. But Carlyle substitutes the hero for the saint ; and

the reorganization that he has in view would be of
a much more secular character.   This is due, however, in the main, to his more deeply humanistic
conception of the nature of religion.   All life is
regarded by him as the working out of great human
ideals ;   and religion simply serves to emphasize
its inmost essence.   " All religion," as he says, " was
here to remind us, better or worse, of the quite
infinite difference there is between a Good man and
a Bad ;   to bid us love infinitely the one, abhor and
avoid infinitely the other—strive infinitely to *be*
the one, and not to be the other."   " The true Shekinah is man " ;   and " all religion issues in due
Practical Hero-worship."   Or, as Swinburne has put
it, with an even more sweeping emphasis—

> " A creed is a rod
> And a crown is of night,
> But this thing is God,
> To be man with thy might,
> To grow straight in the strength of thy spirit, and
> live out thy life as the light."

Carlyle, however, would not altogether agree that
" a crown is of night."   For him, as he says, there
is an " infinite difference between the good man and
the bad," between the hero and him who is not a
hero ;   and the hero is the natural lord over him who
is not.   It is just here, I think, that we see the
fundamental difficulty of Carlyle's humanism, from

the point of view of religion. He who is not a hero
cannot really worship him who is ; he can only, in
the end, be forced into submission. " The eye," as
Carlyle himself is so fond of reminding us, " sees
only what it brings with it the power of seeing " ;
and the eye of him who is not a hero has not the
power of discerning that which is truly heroic. As
William Blake somewhat quaintly put it—

> " Nought loves another as itself,
>   Nor venerates another so,
>   Nor is it possible to thought
>   A greater than itself to know."

At any rate, this would hardly seem to be possible if
the greater is " infinitely different." Accordingly,
the Carlylean hero shows in the end a tendency to
become a despot ; and, indeed, as we have seen,
the power of goodness comes perilously near to a
transformation into the goodness of power—the
very antithesis of humanism. Further, even the
hero has his limitations. He is only in part the
embodiment of the highest human ideal ; and what
is beyond is, for him also, incomprehensible. He
has to be regarded as the instrument or incomplete
expression of a mysterious power beyond himself.
Thus the humanism of Carlyle is at last rounded off
by the recognition of an unknowable something
beyond humanity, a God that " does nothing," a

N

power that can only be accepted as a blind destiny.
In the end one is sometimes tempted to think that
his attitude on the whole matter might be summed
up in his famous reply * to the saying of Margaret
Fuller, that she " accepted the universe "—" Gad !
she'd better ! "

The general attitude of Carlyle, however—the
general conception that " the true Shekinah is man "
—might possibly be restored to its truly humanistic
significance if only we could abolish that " infinite
difference " to which Carlyle refers.   And it might
be urged that human affection is, in reality, quite
capable of transcending such differences ; and that
it is in affection, much more than in worship, that
the ultimate essence of religion lies.   This would
certainly be more in harmony with what seems to be
the fundamental idea of Christianity.   He who was
known as " a friend of publicans and sinners " can
hardly have felt the infinite difference between the
good man and the bad quite in the way in which
Carlyle would appear to conceive it.   Love, it may
be urged, is always, at least in its highest forms,
religious.   It deifies its object, while at the same
time it grasps and comprehends it.   In illustration

* Quoted in James's *Varieties of Religious Experience.*
The saying seems to derive some of its point from the fact that
Carlyle himself, with all his efforts, was never quite able to
" accept the universe."

of this, the utterance of Mr. Kipling's dying girl has been quoted, " There is no God but thee, beloved," and the adaptation of Sappho by Catullus—

> " Ille mi par esse deo videtur,
> Ille, si fas est, superare divos."

To these, indeed, might be added the utterance of Shakespeare's Juliet—

> " Swear by thy gracious self,
> Which is the god of my idolatry."

A poetic " figure of speech " would perhaps be generally recognized in such expressions ; but it has been asked,* in this connection, " Did any man ever love God as he has loved some human beings ? Did he ever derive from the love of God a greater inspiration for all good things and thoughts than from the love of some one or other child of earth ? Did he never feel that in the love of some single human being he was loving God ? " Human affection, however, would seem in itself to be too inconstant and capricious to serve as a real basis for religion. Its object is too purely a creation of the individual heart. It is singled out from other somewhat similar objects around it, and given a more or less factitious value above them, " as the apple tree among the trees of the wood." But this defect can be in large measure removed when human

* By Mr. H. W. Garrod, in *The Religion of all Good Men.*

affection is connected, as in the popular religion of the Japanese, with an established social system, and with a belief in the persistence of its object. It is, then, not merely the love of a person, but the love of a person who endures as a lovable object, and who is part of a living and enduring whole, within which both the lover and the loved are included. Now this, as I take it, is what, in particular, Comte's religion " of humanity " seeks to secure for us, in a form that is not merely national, like the religion of the Japanese, but in the highest degree universal.

The religion of humanity, as conceived by Comte, forms part of a large philosophical system, which, of course, we cannot here consider. But I may sum up what seems to me its significance, as I have done with other positions. It is based on the conception that human history may be conceived as the evolution of a single great being, and that this being should be the ultimate object of our love and reverence. Such a conception removes the great difficulty that appears to be involved in the worship of individuals as such, and presents us with a larger and more abiding object of reverence. It is not easy, however, to render the conception either clear in itself or acceptable as an object of devotion, and especially as an object of love. Love clings to individuals ; and, though humanity may be conceived as a real unity, it can hardly be conceived as an individual unity. Human life, moreover, though it contains the highest that we know in the way of effort and aspiration, is yet, throughout the whole course of its history, a perplexing tangle of good and evil. If we may regard it as the heart of the universe, so far as the universe is known to us, it would yet appear to be a somewhat deceitful heart ; and it would only be the heart of this heart, the *cor cordium,* the inner essence of human progress, that we could really regard as an object of love and reverence. William Blake, in his simple but impressive way, may be said to have anticipated the religion of humanity in his *Songs of Innocence—*

> " To Mercy, Pity, Peace, and Love,
>   All pray in their distress,
>   And to these virtues of delight
>   Return their thankfulness.
>
> " For Mercy, Pity, Peace, and Love,
>   Is God our Father dear ;
>   And Mercy, Pity, Peace, and Love,
>   Is man, his child and care.
>
> " For Mercy has a human heart ;
>   Pity, a human face ;
>   And Love, the human form divine ;
>   And Peace, the human dress.
>
> " Then every man, of every clime,
>   That prays in his distress,
>   Prays to the human form divine :
>   Love, Mercy, Pity, Peace."

But in the *Songs of Experience* he gives us the counter-blast to this—

> "Cruelty has a human heart,
>   And Jealousy a human face ;
> Terror the human form divine,
>   And Secresy the human dress.

> "The human dress is forgèd iron,
>   The human form a fiery forge,
> The human face a furnace sealed,
>   The human heart its hungry gorge."

The same antithesis is more briefly expressed in the older formula—*homo homini deus, homo homini lupus.* We can, it would seem, escape the difficulty to which it calls attention only by the conception of an inner meaning in human life, something that constitutes its essential being, however much it may be obscured in particular manifestations of human life and history. But when we think of humanity in this way, it seems misleading to say that it is humanity as such that we take as the object of our reverence, just as it would be misleading to say that it is the universe that we take as the object of our worship. We single out humanity from the rest of the universe, as containing within it the highest that we know ; but in humanity also we have to make a similar selection of that which is worthy of our devotion. This inner core, the ultimate divine spark, would appear to be what we understand by the supreme good, or the moral ideal ; and thus the religion of humanity would seem in the end to be identified with what has recently been set before us in a simpler and more definite way, as *Ethical Religion.**

Ethical religion I take to be the final expression of the inner meaning of pure humanism in worship. Here at last the second of Kant's great objects of reverence is separated off from all connection with the first. The ideal in man is taken as that which is alone to be supremely valued. The starry heavens and all that they contain, except this pure ideal in the human consciousness, are treated as insignificant and worthless. When, however, we are brought to this extreme point, we can hardly help suspecting that some error has crept into the process by which we have been led to this result. The ideal in the human consciousness is an aspiration after some good to be achieved. The moral life is the effort to realize this good. How can the

---

* This point has been strikingly emphasized by Dr. Stanton Coit in a paper on " Humanity and God " in the *International Journal of Ethics* for July, 1906. The account of the attitude of the positivists there given has, however, (in the following number of the same journal) been vigorously repudiated by Mr. Frederic Harrison, one of the ablest of their leaders. What I have said in the text above seems to me to be substantially true of the attitude and tendency of Comte himself, though perhaps not of all his followers.

aspiration and the effort be of such immeasurable worth if the good to which they are directed is not worthy of our devotion ?   But the good to which they are directed, however we may define it, would seem to be some way in which our lives are brought into right relations to the universe in which they are.   How can these right relations be thought of as of supreme value if the universe itself is regarded as worthless ?

Such questions as this lead us on to the consideration of the limitations of the point of view which we have here described as humanistic.   In religion, more than in any other aspect of life, we see the possibility of concentrating attention on that which is purely human, or what Kant describes as the " good will," and separating that from all reference to the universe in which man is placed.   But it is also in religion, more than in any other aspect of life, that we see in the end the unsatisfactoriness, and indeed the impossibility, of any such separation. Reflection on this may, however, lead us to see that the attempt to set up a pure humanism, in opposition to the study of those objective conditions by which humanity is surrounded, must in reality be futile.   The consideration of this point forms the subject of the next lecture.

LECTURE VIII

LIMITATIONS OF HUMANISM

WE have now seen, in general terms, what is to be understood by humanism, and we have considered how it may be applied in several of the most important aspects of life. The significance of it lies mainly in its emphasis on those conceptions of purpose, quality, value, which in our ordinary study of nature we can conveniently ignore—just as, in studying grammar, it does not matter whether the sentences that we select for analysis are those of Shakespeare or of Martin Tupper. When, however, we are studying the higher aspects of life, it becomes necessary to reintroduce those conceptions which had been, for the sake of convenience, omitted. The ways in which this may be done have now, I think, been sufficiently illustrated; and it remains for us to ask with what qualifications, if any, the use of these conceptions is to be regarded as valid.

In order to bring this out, I must remind you of what was stated in the first lecture with

regard to the different senses in which humanism may be understood. It was there explained
that there are a large number of different
interpretations of the term, but that there
are, in particular, three distinguishable meanings
that it seems important to recognize. The first
sense is that in which it simply means that special
emphasis is to be laid on the study of human life,
and that we must try to study it in such a method
as is specially appropriate to it. It is in this sense,
as we saw, that Socrates may be taken as the
typical humanist. It is hardly possible, however,
to rest here. Any one who aims at a scientific
method in the study of the world can hardly separate off man's life from other things, and treat it
in a way that is exclusively its own. It seems clear
that man is, in some sense, a part of a larger whole ;
and that he can only be properly understood in
relation to that whole. Hence we are almost inevitably led on from this first interpretation of
humanism to some kind of theory that maintains
that the world as a whole is to be interpreted from
the human standpoint. But this again may either
mean that the world, so far as it seems to be contrasted with human life, is to be somehow explained
away, as being an illusion, an appearance, or something of which nothing can be known, and which is

of no intrinsic importance ; or it may mean rather
that the world is to be regarded as having a certain
reality and importance of its own, but that it must
ultimately be interpreted in relation to human life.

Now, what I seek to maintain is that the last of
these interpretations is the only one that can ultimately be accepted as scientifically satisfactory.
In this sense, however, the term almost loses its
more specific meaning. It almost ceases to be
opposed to naturalism ; since it seeks to include
the facts of the natural world, and to give them
a place as aspects of reality, though subordinating
them to conceptions derived from the study of
human life. Hence, when humanism is used as a
descriptive title for a philosophical theory, it
tends to be used more nearly in the second of the
three meanings that have been referred to—i.e. as
referring to a view which, in some way or other,
emphasizes the study of human life almost to the
exclusion of other aspects of reality. Of course,
it is evident that this may be done in very varying
degrees ; and we cannot really make any sharp
distinction between the second and the third interpretation. But my point in the present lecture
is to urge that there is a constant danger of re-
lapsing into some more or less pronounced form of
the second interpretation ; and that it is of great

importance that we should constantly bear in mind
that it is some form of the third interpretation at
which we have to aim.

What I wish to bring forward in the present lecture
is, in short, that, valuable as the humanistic conceptions are, it would be a fatal mistake to suppose
that they can be taken as complete in themselves,
when they are understood in the sense in which
they are contrasted with the other aspects of our
experience. Indeed, I would even urge that, when
they are interpreted in this way, they cease to be
truly humanistic, and take on to a large extent the
character of that from which we are trying to distinguish them. A simple illustration may serve
to bring out my general meaning in this. What,
let me ask, is a "humanitarian," and what is a
"cynic"? A humanitarian is not one who constantly distinguishes man from all other beings
and is proud of his superiority, but rather one
who constantly recognizes that the lower animals
are his poor relations. The Cynics, on the other
hand, were so named from their bestial mode of
life,* a mode of life which arose from the attempt to
ignore all external conditions, and to assert the
pure inner ideal. "Man," Tennyson tells us, "is

* The Cynics, however, had their revenge. It was largely
through the influence of their stoical successors that our word
"humane" acquired its modern meaning.

not as God, but then most godlike being most a man."
Man, we might almost add, is not a beast, but then
most bestial when he forgets his kinship with the
brutes, and with the general system of nature from
which he springs. The attempt to live a life in
which the animal nature of man and the external
conditions of his existence are set aside, nearly
always leads to a result which is strictly inhuman.
This may serve to call our attention to the fact that
we cannot really separate off human life from the
rest of the universe, as a thing that is to be understood entirely in its own light, and in comparison
with which everything else may be neglected;
and this is, in general, the qualification that I now
wish to make upon the humanistic point of view.
In order to make this more explicit, it may be convenient, in dealing with it, to pursue the same order
as before, and bring out the limitations of humanism
(1) in philosophy, (2) in politics, (3) in economics
(4) in education, and (5) in religion.

(1) *In Philosophy.*—Pure humanism in philosophy, if we were to state it briefly in the form in
which the opinions of the early Greek philosophers
are commonly (I think somewhat unfairly) summarized, would be the doctrine that " all is man." *

---

* Or " all is mind," as in the philosophy of Berkeley. It is
remarkable how largely what is called idealism in this country

Now, the whole tendency of philosophical development has certainly gone to show that such a doctrine would furnish us with a more adequate theory of the universe than " all is water," or " all is fire," or " all is number," or " all is atoms and the void," or (to take more modern equivalents) " all is electricity," or " all is matter in motion." But most of us have learned (perhaps even the early Greek philosophers had learned) that it is not very satisfactory to attempt to sum up the universe in such phrases. And the more definitely we pass from naturalistic to humanistic interpretations, the more inadequate do such summary phrases appear. Man can hardly be supposed to be a simple element, as water or number or electricity may at first seem to be. If we say that man is

(even when ostensibly based on the positions of Kant and Hegel) continues to be coloured by the views of Berkeley. The type of idealism, for instance, which is set forth in Dr. McTaggart's recent book, *Some Dogmas of Religion*, seems to me to be almost purely Berkeleyan throughout. The same is in some degree true of the doctrines set forth in Haldane's *Pathway to Reality* and several other recent works. In connection with any such theories, one can but wonder what sort of thing a mind would be without any world for it to apprehend. Idealism of this type was almost sufficiently refuted by Kant. Yet it is still often supposed that all idealism is of this character. Those who think so can hardly have made much acquaintance with such an idealism as that of the Master of Balliol. (See, for instance, his book on *The Evolution of Theology in the Greek Philosophers*, especially Lecture XII.)

the key to the universe, we are, at any rate, acknowledging that the key is a somewhat complicated one. Hence it is not surprising that Anaxagoras, who may fairly be claimed as the first of the humanists, did not put forward his *νοῦς* as a complete explanation of the universe, but only as that which gives order and coherence to what would otherwise be a chaotic mass. The more definitely humanistic philosophers, Plato and Aristotle, were disposed, as we have already noticed, to criticize Anaxagoras on this account. But " wisdom is justified of all her children " ; and it is by no means certain that Anaxagoras could not be very well defended against these attacks. It might even be urged that he had, in some respects, a more adequate conception than his critics of what is required for a complete theory of reality.*

At any rate, when Plato and Aristotle tried on their own account to give a more definitely humanistic theory of the universe their efforts can hardly be held to have been completely successful, great and admirable though they undoubtedly were. Plato takes the idea of the Good as the ultimate source of all reality, and seeks to range under it all the subordinate types. But even this attempt is

* Cf. the comments by W. Wallace in the article " Anaxagoras " in the ninth edition of the *Encyclopædia Britannica*.

never definitely carried out ; and in the end we seem to find, over against the world of ideas, a refractory material, which also must be in some sense real. The good has to struggle against ἀνάγκη, and the subordinate types have to find their embodiment in the ὑποδοχή of space. Yet of these opposing elements there is no explanation. If the failure of Aristotle is not quite so conspicuous, this is partly due to the fact that he does not attempt so much. In his efforts to deal with the various special philosophical sciences—with logic, psychology, ethics, politics, etc.—he is in general brilliantly successful ; and one almost forgets, in reading his discussions on these subjects, that the more ultimate problems remain unsolved. The recognition of the two fundamental determinants—ὕλη and εἶδος— can hardly be supposed to furnish us with any real explanation of the concrete universe ; and, in any case, the kind of explanation that it suggests is a dualistic, not a purely humanistic, explanation.* And the same fundamental difficulty that we find in Plato and Aristotle seems still to haunt us in the work of their modern disciple, Leibniz. With him also we find, over against the conception of the Good, the limiting ideas of *materia prima* and the " in-

---

* These points are brought out, with great thoroughness, in Caird's *Evolution of Theology in the Greek Philosophers.*

compossibility " of certain positive qualities, which do not appear to have any real explanation in the idea of the Good itself.

Berkeley may be taken as, in many respects, a more thorough type of the pure humanist in philosophy than any of these. What we call the external world is, for him, only a system of ideas in the minds of thinking persons. This view, however, rests on the supposition that thinking beings can know nothing but their own ideas ; and, as soon as this presupposition is clearly realized, we find ourselves landed in the absolute scepticism of Hume, for whom real persons can be just as little apprehended as real things.

What has in recent times been called pragmatism is another instance of a purely humanistic movement in philosophy. This has, of course, its ancient analogue in the point of view of Protagoras, summed up in the saying that " man is the measure of all things." The Protagorean position, so far as it can be gathered from the accounts that have come down to us, does not involve, like Berkeley's, that there is no reality beyond that which is contained in the consciousness of thinking beings, but only that it is not possible for any one to transcend the point of view of the individual consciousness in the apprehension of theoretical truth. It seems doubtful

o

whether Protagoras was prepared to deny the possibility of objective distinctions in the apprehension of good and evil. Modern pragmatism, on the other hand, connects the theoretical and the practical aspects of life more closely, maintaining that in both cases we are ultimately concerned with an act of individual choice. Now, if we are at all right in our previous defence of the humanistic position, we must recognize an element of truth in this contention. Truth, like goodness, is certainly a human ideal. It would never come to us if we did not, in some sense, " will to believe " it ; and perhaps it is true to say also that all human beliefs must be of the nature of working hypotheses. But there we must pause, if we are not to land ourselves in an absolute scepticism. If we are to avoid this result —a result that we can hardly " will to believe "— we must try to maintain two things—(1) that our choice, whether in theory or in practice, is not merely an individual choice, but is guided by universal principles, so that it may truly be said to be the choice of man ; (2) that this human point of view is not an arbitrary one, but grows up in relation to the objective conditions by which man's life is determined, and involves a genuine (if limited) apprehension of the nature of these conditions. Now, on these points, the trumpet of the prag-

matists—in general, not deficient in loudness—
seems to give an uncertain sound. But everything
turns on the view that is to be taken with regard
to them. Pure humanism, which simply takes its
stand on the fact of choice, the adventure of the
individual soul, the pious wager, without consideration of the conditions by which the choice is determined and justified, leads us to a position that is
essentially sceptical. The confidence of the individual chooser, however noble and heroic it may
seem to himself, must inevitably, in such circumstances, appear as a wilful blindness to the critical
onlooker. On the other hand, if we recognize the
universality and objectivity of our choice, and
proceed to vindicate it by a reference to the conditions on which it depends, we have ceased to be
pure humanists, and cannot surely, in any case,
be properly described as pragmatists.

The objectivity of the conditions of rational
belief is the point that is specially brought home to
us by those who are commonly characterized as
the new realists ; and, whatever we may think of
their views in themselves, they seem at least to
have done valuable service in emphasizing the
limitations of humanism. The modern realist
directs his attack mainly against what is commonly
called " subjective idealism " ; and, more indirectly,

against that form of scepticism which is the inevitable outcome of the subjective position. He urges that the world that we know is not simply, or indeed at all, a world in our heads, but is rather, from the first and throughout, a world of objects by reference to which alone the ideas in our minds can be made intelligible. This contention tells mainly against the philosophies of Berkeley and Hume; but it also tells in the end against all forms of pure humanism, i.e. against all attempts to understand man's life purely from within, without reference to the objective world which it is his constant aim to grasp and interpret.*

Indeed, even in the attempt to study the growth of the human consciousness itself, it is not really possible to adopt a purely introspective attitude. This has been, more and more, brought out by the development of recent psychology. Considerable efforts have been made, even in quite recent times, to represent psychology as a purely introspective science; and, in particular, the doctrine of psychophysical parallelism has been eagerly seized upon as an instrument for rendering such treatment

* The points here briefly indicated are brought out, somewhat more fully, in a paper on "The New Realism and the Old Idealism" in *Mind*, July, 1906.

possible, and even giving it an air of reasonableness:* According to this doctrine, the facts of consciousness are so entirely disparate to the physical and physiological conditions with which they are connected, that no real relation can be established between the two sets of facts. Hence the facts of consciousness must be treated as a world by themselves, revealed to us by pure introspection, and incapable of any other mode of treatment. But the artificiality of this separation is, more and more, coming to be recognized by psychologists ; and it is rapidly being dropped in their practice, however it may linger in their theory. We have already made some attempt to bring out the real significance of the underlying contention. The point is that changes in consciousness are not capable of being explained by reference to the mechanical movements which precede or accompany them ; and this certainly seems to be undeniable. They are not simply modes of mechanical movement. But it is also true that all qualitative changes, whether of heat, electricity, life, or anything else that we know, are equally in-

---

* It is enough to refer to such handbooks as those of Höffding and Stout. In view of some of Professor Stout's more recent writings, I should suppose that he would hardly now maintain the view that is put forward in his *Manual*—though even that involves a considerable modification of the doctrine of psychophysical parallelism, as ordinarily understood.

capable of explanation on that basis ; and it does not appear to be the case that what is qualitatively distinctive in these cases can be resolved into modes of consciousness. The facts of consciousness, then, it would seem, are capable of just as much and just as little explanation by means of mechanical movements as any other facts of a qualitative character. And, indeed, this is what, in their practice, all psychologists recognize. They make no attempt to explain the facts of consciousness by mechanical movements ; but they do, nevertheless, account for changes in consciousness—especially for the introduction of new sensations—by reference to their physical and physiological conditions.*

The view then to which, on general philosophical grounds, we appear to be led is briefly this : that in the study of human life we have to take full account of that element of quality which, in dealing with

---

* Valuable discussions bearing on these points are to be found in Ward's *Naturalism and Agnosticism* and Taylor's *Elements of Metaphysics*. With the latter, in particular, I find myself in substantial agreement. The attempts of Sir Oliver Lodge, in his book on *Life and Matter*, to bring out the relations between consciousness and energy, though also very interesting, seem to me much more open to question. His conception of life as a special kind of force entering into the material system *ab extra* hardly seems to be philosophically tenable. How far his conception of guidance meets the purely physical difficulties I am not really qualified to judge. It seems clear, however, that any view of the system of the universe which does not leave some place for conscious control must be incomplete.

the rest of the universe, we may generally ignore, or treat as of second-rate importance ; but that, in fact, this element cannot be entirely eliminated from the rest of the universe ; nor can the life of man be thoroughly dealt with without a full recognition of the mechanical conditions under which that life, as we know it, has always to be passed. The modern doctrine of evolution has, of course, specially brought home to us this intimate connection between man and the world below him ; but it was, in truth, recognized to the full by Aristotle and many of the older thinkers, and can hardly indeed be ignored by any one who has an eye for the facts, however in words he may seek to deny it. We may maintain, as emphatically as we will, that man is, in quality, immeasurably above everything else that we know ; we may extol him as the finest flower of creation ; but we cannot understand his life without giving careful attention to the soil and climate of the garden in which he is reared.

(2) *In Politics.*—After this general statement of the point of view from which human life is to be regarded, it can hardly be necessary to dwell at any length on its particular application to the study of politics. It is evident that it would be vain to set up a qualitative ideal as the goal of human endeavour if the advance to it did not belong, in some

degree, to the nature of human life. It would then be mere quixotism. If the " moral order " and the " cosmic order "—to use Huxley's antithesis—were hopelessly opposed, there could be no real philosophy of the political life. A mere " ought to be," which all the conditions of human development resisted, could hardly even be recognized as an " ought." If, for instance, the progress of the race were only possible through the perpetuation of a blind struggle for existence, it would be vain to try to ameliorate human conditions by the introduction of mutual help. It is perhaps chiefly in this respect that the political philosophy of Aristotle shows a marked advance on that of Plato. The Platonic state exists " in heaven "—i.e. nowhere ; it is an almost pure ideal, only very loosely connected with the conditions of human life as we know it. Aristotle, on the other hand, though constantly guided, no less than Plato, by an ideal aim, yet constantly seeks to show that his ideal is realizable on earth. To do this is, however, a much more difficult task. It involves, in modern phraseology, the conviction that evolution may become truly " orthogenic," or " aristogenic " ; that human choice can be gradually substituted for the blind selection of animal struggle. But it seems clear that, in any case, this substitution can only be a gradual one ;

and how far it is possible at all can only be determined by a study of the organic conditions of human life.*

(3) *In Economics.*—What has to be said with regard to the still more special aspect of economics must of course be very similar. Here we might take such a writer as Ruskin as the representative of pure humanism. The defects of his position I have already tried to indicate. Values cannot be determined purely from within, or simply by references to human ends that can be directly ascertained. The changing conditions of our environment—due, no doubt, in part to the gradual evolution of man's own life, but in part also to real alterations in his material circumstances, and to modifications in the relations between him and them—have to be constantly taken into account. The changes, moreover, which values in this way undergo, can in general only be estimated in an indirect and somewhat mechanical fashion. It may be doubted whether it would be possible to devise any real method of determining them, without reference to those brute facts of demand and supply with which the purely analytical economist is mainly

---

* Such difficulties, for instance, as those brought forward in Haycraft's *Darwinism and Race Progress* would have to be carefully considered.

concerned. And there are many other ways in which it must be recognized by the economist that the conditions that he has to study are largely determined by a struggle for existence, in which the best does not always survive. It is not only bad money that, as we are taught by " Gresham's Law," tends to drive out good. Against such tendencies, no doubt, we have to struggle ; here the more ethical economists are right. But it is vain to struggle against them by any direct resistance, and still more vain to ignore them. We must recognize them as we recognize gravitation or friction, and evade their evil consequences by understanding their action. When we thoroughly understand them, we may even be able to use them, as we can use gravitation or friction, as the instruments of our progress.

(4) *In Education.*—With regard to education also I have already to a considerable extent indicated what I conceive to be the limitations of humanism. I have conceded the necessity of scientific studies, and have even allowed that they ought perhaps to have the priority. A purely humanistic education would, as Plato put it, result in the production of the " too musical man," who understands, perhaps, some of the highest aspirations of the soul, but is ill prepared to grapple with the conditions through which

their realization has to be striven for. Plato seeks accordingly, to supplement this side, in the first instance, by gymnastics and military drill. Certainly a training, like that of Cromwell's Ironsides, might be of considerable value, not merely to those who have to contend for kingdoms, but to those who have to struggle for any kind of social advancement. All human effort requires fortitude and self-restraint. But scientific studies, as Plato seems to have partly realized later, serve to some extent a similar purpose ; and so, indeed, do the more mechanical aspects of linguistic studies. Browning's " grammarian " had certainly cultivated fortitude and self-restraint. And, at any rate, we may safely affirm that, in some form or other, an exact knowledge of the chief mechanical conditions of life, and a readiness to deal with them, are essential elements in any complete education. Even the fine arts, it must be remembered, rest to some extent on the mechanical ones ; and beauty has at least one of its roots in utility. For these reasons one ought, I think, to be somewhat chary of offering a too strenuous opposition to the utilitarian and technical tendencies of modern educational developments. What is wanted, rather, is not to resist the utilitarian spirit, but to guide it towards ampler ends ; and especially to substitute a qualitative conception of the wellbeing that is aimed at for the somewhat blind accumulation of the mechanical instruments of happiness.

(5) *In Religion.*—Finally, we return to the problem of religion, in which we have already, to some extent, seen that too pure a humanism carries us into the region of empty abstraction. I need not here emphasize the impossibility of making human life the sole object of our reverence, in view of its intrinsic smallness in comparison with the universe of which it is a part. This is, indeed, a point that the religious consciousness is continually forced to feel. What, it may be asked, are even the greatest men that we know—Shakespeare, Aristotle, Julius Cæsar, and others ; nay, what are even those mythical or semi-mythical heroes, whom the world has been prepared to worship—Buddha, Christ, Hercules, and the like—in comparison with what we may imagine of the types of life that may be realized in the innumerable larger worlds that are scattered through the abysses of space ? I do not dwell on this ; for, after all, human life is the highest mode of existence that we actually know ; and we must not allow ourselves to be imposed upon by the merely quantitative infinite. But, acknowledging that human life is our highest object of reverence, we may still ask whether it is really possible to

separate the pure soul of man from the bodily conditions in connection with which it is developed.
The soul, so far as we know, cannot subsist *in vacuo*.
Even Browning, who is in the main the poet of the
human soul, teaches us to recognize its bodily
accompaniments.

> " Let us not always say
> 'Spite of this flesh to-day
> I strove, made head, gained ground upon the whole!'
> As the bird wings and sings,
> Let us cry 'All good things
> Are ours, nor soul helps flesh more, now, than flesh helps
> soul!'"

More definitely, we may put the point in the following way. We have seen that pure humanism in
religion leads in the end to the worship of the moral
ideal. But if the moral ideal is to have any real significance for us, it must at least have some positive
content. It must mean the realization of happiness,
or of some type of desirable human life, or of something else, in Aristotle's phrase, that can be done
and achieved by man. Now this seems to involve,
in the end, that it must somehow be in harmony
with the inner spirit of the universe within which
man's life is spent. Otherwise it may prove a mere
empty conceit. I do not mean, of course, that the
moral life must be thought of as leading to success
in any vulgar or external sense. Its only glory

may be that of " going on." Prometheus bound may even be our ultimate type of what is highest. But, at any rate, if we are to think of it as great and admirable and worthy of worship, we can hardly suppose it to be a mere piece of human self-assertion. It must show insight into the real nature of things, and be in essential harmony with that nature.

Perhaps I may bring out more clearly what I mean by taking an illustration from literature. Mr. A. C. Bradley, in his recent book on *Shakespearean Tragedy*, has brought powerfully before us the significance of the play of *King Lear* as a great religious drama, which has to be grouped " with works like the *Prometheus Vinctus* and the *Divine Comedy*, and even with the greatest symphonies of Beethoven, and the statues in the Medici Chapel." Yet in hardly any other play does human life seem to be represented as so pitiable a failure.

> " As flies to wanton boys are we to the gods ;
>   They kill us for their sport."

And, in general, the types of life there depicted seem hardly fit for anything but killing. " This is certainly," says Mr. Bradley, " the most terrible picture that Shakespeare painted of the world. In no other of his tragedies does humanity appear more pitiably infirm or more hopelessly bad." We seem reduced to the most absolute pessimism, and ask ourselves—" Is it not Shakespeare's judgment on his kind that we hear in Lear's appeal—

> ' And thou, all shaking thunder,
> Smite flat the thick rotundity o' the world !
> Crack nature's moulds, all germens spill at once,
> That make ungrateful man ! '

and Shakespeare's judgment on the worth of existence that we hear in Lear's agonized cry, ' No, no, no life ! ' ? " But Mr. Bradley maintains, rightly or wrongly, that this is not to be taken as the last word of King Lear ; and he brings out the other side in a way that is very impressive. He says, of the death of King Lear, that, " though he is killed by an agony of pain, the agony in which he actually dies is one not of pain but of ecstasy. Suddenly, with a cry represented in the oldest text by a four-times repeated ' O,' he exclaims—

> ' Do you see this ?   Look on her, look, her lips,
> Look there, look there ! '

These are the last words of Lear.   He is sure, at last, that she *lives ;* and what had he said when he was still in doubt ?

> ' She lives ! if it be so,
> It is a chance which does redeem all sorrows
> That ever I have felt ! ' "

Now, it is not for me to attempt to determine here
whether this interpretation of *King Lear* is correct ;
but it may serve at least as an illustration of what I
mean. The one thing that redeems the horror of
the play is the truthfulness of Cordelia—a simple
human excellence, in the midst of storms, brutality,
and madness. This excellence certainly, in all
ordinary senses of the word, fails. It fails partly
because it is not sufficiently accompanied by other
excellences. It not only does not accomplish its
object ; it is misunderstood, and is a source of end-
less disasters, culminating in the death of its posses-
sor and of all that is most dear to her ; for it is only
the last and most pathetic of Lear's delusions if he
thinks she " lives." Yet I believe it is true that
Shakespeare means us to find a profound consolation
—surely, at least, a great significance—in these
closing words—

> "Look on her, look, her lips,
> Look there, look there ! "

He means, I believe, to hint at least—though with
all the subtle reticence of the highest art—that
there is some sense in which the truthfulness
of her lips may be held to vanquish disaster
and death. What is that sense ? That I do not
here undertake to explain ; but I think it must

at least imply that human fidelity is something more deeply rooted in the nature of things than the stupidity and brutality in the midst of which it appears to be overwhelmed. It is not merely something that we choose or value, but something that, from the point of view of the universe, is greatest and deepest and most triumphant. This seems to me to be, in the end, the essence of all true religion ; and, if so, it is not merely humanistic, in any sense that implies an ultimate antithesis between man's ideals and the universe in which they have to be realized.

P

LECTURE IX

IMPLICATIONS OF HUMANISM

IT has been my object, in the foregoing lectures, to bring out the general significance of the point of view from which human life may be regarded as containing the key to the universe, or at least as containing the key to itself; to illustrate some of the more concrete applications of this point of view; and, at the same time, to indicate that we cannot really sever the life of man from that of the universe of which he is part, or ignore his dependence on the conditions by which he is surrounded. This view I have only been able, in these lectures, to illustrate and emphasize in a somewhat sketchy fashion, not to prove or develop with any thoroughness; nor is it possible for me now to make good this deficiency. Evidently the view to which I have been referring implies a complete metaphysical theory of the universe; and it would be utterly futile to attempt to work out any such theory here. Nor, indeed, can it be thought altogether necessary that I should do so. The general position to which we are led is that which is commonly described by the term idealism, in the sense in which that term is applied to Plato among the ancients and to Hegel among the moderns, as distinguished from that in which it may be applied to Malebanche or to Berkeley. This point of view has been brought home to us, and more or less successfully adapted to our British modes of thought and expression, by such diverse exponents as Edward Caird, F. H. Bradley, and James Ward—to mention only three of the most distinguished among many. Though these writers differ widely from one another,* yet there are certain fundamental conceptions that they possess in common ; and if they have not been successful in making these conceptions clear and convincing,

---

* They differ, I think, both in the ways in which they habitually approach the subject and in the general character of the conclusions that they present. Caird approaches from the point of view of the sympathetic appreciation of the philosophic thought of all the ages, showing its origin, its truth, its defects, and the direction in which it leads. Bradley is, above all, a dialectician, bringing out the inadequacy of all points of view except the highest, the nature of which he is perhaps less successful in unfolding. Ward presents himself mainly as the critic of the point of view commonly associated with the physical sciences. In results, Ward tends to emphasize the conscious life and volition of the individual, while Bradley seems in general to lose the individual in the whole. The view of Caird seems to be more successful than either of the others in balancing these opposite sides. On the other hand, his treatment, being largely historical, does not perhaps lend itself to quite so definite a summing up of the final outcome. His positive conclusions are to be found chiefly in his works dealing with theology and religion.

I certainly could not hope to help them. I have, however, been approaching the subject in a somewhat peculiar fashion, partly on account of the nature of the course that I have had to deliver, as bearing upon sociological questions, and partly on account of the way in which the problems have happened to appeal to me ; and I believe it may not be unprofitable, in this closing lecture, to bring out, somewhat more fully than I have yet been able to do, the ultimate implications of the position that I have been trying to expound ; and, if possible, to remove some of the difficulties that naturally present themselves in connection with it.

The following are the points upon which I intend to touch. First of all, it seems necessary to add a little more by way of elucidating more fully those fundamental conceptions of quality and end which underlie everything that I have been trying to put before you. This will lead us naturally to a further consideration of the view of causation which seems to be implied in the use of the conception of end. In close connection with this, some difficulties suggest themselves with regard to the nature of time ; and I must at least endeavour to indicate how I conceive that these difficulties may be removed. It will then be possible to sum up briefly

the general conception of ultimate reality to which
we are led. Some further difficulties, however, at
once present themselves at this stage with regard to
the distinction between good and evil ; and these
also must be summarily dealt with. Finally, I
intend to indicate the sort of proof of which I conceive that such a doctrine of the universe is susceptible.

(1) *On Quality.*—It is evident that the conception
of quality lies at the basis of the general point of
view that I have here put forward. Now, this
conception has, on the whole, been almost entirely
ignored throughout the greater part of the history of
philosophy. This has been due in the main to a
straining after unity and simplicity. The early Greek
philosophers sought to eliminate all distinctions of
quality, in order that they might be able to explain
the universe by means of one simple element.
Similarly, the Cartesians sought to eliminate them,
in order that their two simple substances might each
have only one essential attribute. Kant gives a place
to what he calls categories of quality ; but his treatment of the subject is very significant of the way in
which the conception has been disregarded. He first
of all identifies quality, for all practical purposes,
with degree, or intensive magnitude, which he calls
its schema. Then he appears even to suggest that

intensive magnitude can be treated as reducible to extensive magnitude.* Quality, in the proper sense, he refuses to recognize as a conception that is capable of philosophical treatment.† It is only to

* This seems to me to be involved in his view that the " anticipations of perception " are " constitutive." " The principles," he says, " which we considered before (i.e. the ' axioms of intuition ' and ' anticipations of perception '), and which, as they enable us to apply mathematics to phenomena, I called mathematical, refer to phenomena so far only as they are possible, and showed how, with regard both to their intuition and to the real in their perception, they can be produced according to the rules of a mathematical synthesis, so that, in the one as well as in the other, we may use numerical quantities, and with them a determination of all phenomena as quantities. Thus I might, for example, compound the degree of sensations of the sunlight out of, say, 200,000 illuminations by the moon, and thus determine it a priori or construct it, (*Critique of Pure Reason*, " Analogies of Experience," Max Müller's translation). Kant, of course wrote at a time when nothing was known of the Weber-Fechner Law and its implications ; but, even apart from this, such a statement as the above is certainly somewhat startling, and is hardly intelligible except as a residual effect of the older doctrine, which Kant did much to destroy, that all the determinations of objects are reducible to terms of extensive magnitude. I ought, perhaps, to add here that I do not mean to deny that degrees may be *enumerated*, and in that way given a quasi-extensive interpretation. See, for instance, Stout's *Manual of Psychology*, p. 31, Rashdall's *Theory of Good and Evil*, vol. ii.. pp. 25–6, and Bradley's paper on the intensity of psychical states (*Mind*, New Series, vol. iv.). But such considerations do not seem to imply any real possibility of transmuting intensive determinations into extensive.

† " The quality of sensation, colour, taste, etc., is always empirical, and cannot even be conceived a priori " (" Anticipations of Perception "). Is it any more " empirical," we naturally ask, than, for instance, the three dimensions of space ?

be accepted as an empirical fact, presented to us in the data of sense. Yet surely we make use of quality, quite as truly as we make use of quantity or degree, or any of the other conceptions that are recognized by Kant, in the determination of the world of our experience. But it would be difficult to point to any philosophical writer who has adequately brought this out. The distinction so often drawn between primary and secondary qualities has tended very largely to obscure it. The primary qualities, which have been supposed to be alone objective in their significance, are essentially quantitative in character. Qualities, in the distinctive sense of the word, have consequently been treated as purely subjective. But there seems to be no real basis for this distinction, at least in the form in which it is commonly put forward.* All that we apprehend of the world, whether primary or secondary, must be apprehended through subjective affections ; but it is all built up, though no doubt in very different ways, into our objective construction of the world. The world, as we know it, is certainly a world that contains qualitative differences. We

---

* Professor Stout has done much to clear up the distinction between primary and secondary qualities, especially in a paper read before the Aristotelean Society and published in its *Proceedings* (New Series, vol. iv.). See also Taylor's *Elements of Metaphysics*, pp. 128–31. But much still remains to be done.

do not create for ourselves the distinctions between colours, sounds, and the like. They come to us; they belong to the world that we apprehend, though their exact place in that world may be difficult to determine. This, then, is the first point that it seems necessary to recognize. The universe that we know possesses, among its most distinctive and irreducible features, certain qualitative differences.*

(2) *On Teleology.*—The conception of end connects very closely with that of quality. In the case of extensive magnitudes, the distinguishable elements stand side by side as equal parts or components of a whole. In degree, we have a scale of distinguishable experiences proceeding upwards from zero to some assignable point. In the case of quality, there is no such simple order of arrangement; but, if we are to group distinguishable qualities in any definite system at all, it seems necessary to arrange them in some order of merit or preferability. We say that one quality is better or higher than another. At any rate, the conception of preferability seems to involve differences of quality, and very easily connects itself with the conception

* Ward's *Naturalism and Agnosticism* is perhaps the book that most thoroughly brings out the inadequacy of quantitative determinations; but the positive nature of qualitative determinations is but slightly indicated in it. This whole subject seems to stand greatly in need of a much fuller investigation than any that it has yet received.

of qualitative difference. But when we arrange things in an order of preferability we imply an end, standard, or ideal, by reference to which one thing is judged to be preferable to another. Thus the conception of end is almost inseparable from that of quality.

Now, the conception of end also has been somewhat hardly dealt with by philosophy in general, and especially by modern philosophy. Here again, as we have seen, it is a stone which the Cartesian builders, before the time of Leibniz, persistently rejected. Leibniz introduced it *ab extra*, in a way that harmonized but ill with the other conceptions with which he worked. Kant almost excludes it even from his ethical system, and gives it only a precarious footing in his *Critique of Judgment*. Some later philosophers have no doubt given it a position of more importance ; but it remains true on the whole that the conception of end, like that of quality, has never yet had justice done to it by modern philosophers.* In general, it tends to be regarded, like quality, as purely subjective in its significance. Kant, for instance—who has so largely set the tone of recent philosophical thinking—

---

* In quite recent times this is, no doubt, ceasing to be true. In particular, the works of Professor Ward, Royce, and Taylor have done much to place this conception on a more satisfactory footing.

treats the conception of end as one that is legitimate
and even necessary in all human efforts to interpret
life and beauty, but not as one that can be accepted
as having a real objective significance in the determination of the universe that we know.　But this
view results largely from Kant's artificial method
of arriving at his categories.　A few conceptions,
somewhat arbitrarily—one might almost say fan-
tastically—connected with the forms of the logical
judgment are taken by him as those that are alone
valid for the determination of the knowable universe.
Among these end does not happen to be included ;
nor, indeed, properly speaking, does quality, though
it is included in name.　Once we recognize the
arbitrariness of Kant's method, we may be prepared to allow that the conception of end has quite
as much right as any of the others with which he
deals to be taken as an objective determination of
the universe.

It is no doubt true that the conception of end is,
in a very special sense, a human category.　This is
true in the sense that I have been seeking to bring
out in the foregoing lectures.　It is only in the study
of human life that the conception of end is necessarily put in the forefront of our treatment ; and
any treatment in which it is prominent may, consequently, be described as humanistic.　But this

must not be taken to mean that it is merely subjective. In qualification of any such restriction, we have first to remember—what, of course, even Kant emphasizes—that it is a necessary form of human thought, not an arbitrary invention of any individual consciousness. Besides this, we must observe—what Kant also allows—that it does not really seem to be possible to interpret even the animal consciousness without supposing that there is some implicit determination by ends. From the animal consciousness, again, it is an easy step to the animal subconsciousness and to processes of a purely physiological character; and along this line we seem to be inevitably led—still with Kant as our guide or companion—to the recognition that all organic life has to be interpreted, in some degree, in the light of this conception. But to recognize so much is in effect to say that it is an objective determination of the universe that we know, though it may be only in the human mind that it comes to any definite consciousness of itself, and so becomes an explicitly controlling force.

(3) *On Causation.*—If, however, we recognize ends as determining factors in the real world, it is clear that we must, in some degree, modify the ordinary conception of causation ; and this also I have endeavoured to explain in the foregoing lectures.

But some further comments may be useful at this point. The fact is that the ordinary conception of causation has been completely subverted by the progress of the sciences ; so that it is hardly necessary to attack it with philosophical criticism. The ordinary conception of causation is that of efficiency. The cause is supposed to put forth a certain inherent energy, by means of which it brings about the effect. How this energy is exerted—for instance, in the case of the attraction between the heavenly bodies —is admitted by common sense to be something of a mystery ; but it is commonly supposed that we are, at any rate, directly conscious of this putting forth of energy in the case of the activity of our own wills. Now, Hume was, I think, perfectly successful in showing that the action of the will is not in reality any more intelligible to us, on the supposition of an inherent energy put forth, than is any other event in nature. With regard to the ordinary events of nature, the modern scientific conception recognizes a certain continuity of motion (more definitely expressed in the doctrine of the conservation of energy) ; and, as regards qualitative changes, knows of nothing but regularity of sequence. This is, of course, the view for the definite establishment of which Hume is mainly responsible, and which was in essence adopted by

Kant.* Now, what the conception of teleology adds to this is the suggestion that qualitative differences—and perhaps, in the end, quantitative relations as well—may be interpreted by means of what Plato called the " idea of the good." This suggestion is, of course, derived, in the first instance, from what we know of human action. We seem compelled to interpret man's life by reference to the fact of choice ; and this seems to contain in it a more or less clearly defined conception of an end. This mode of interpretation, again, as I have already indicated, is almost inevitably extended to the treatment of the animal consciousness, in which also the idea of end would seem to be implicit. We are thus very naturally led to extend the conception to the interpretation of the universe in general ; and there appears to be no real reason why we should not do so. It is especially a way in which the qualitative aspects of the universe can be made more intelligible to us. Such an application of the conception of end does not necessarily mean that we should attempt—as Plato claimed from Anaxagoras—to explain everything directly by showing that it exists for the best. We may,

* Kant's refutation of Hume had reference only to the a priori and necessary character of the conception of causation, not to the nature of the conception itself, which he, like Hume, thought of simply as containing the idea of a certain regularity of sequence.

on the contrary, continue to use all the four Aristotelean causes as useful for purposes of explanation. Continuity of motion, as studied in the purely physical sciences, would correspond to the material cause. A certain definite order in the kinds and qualities of things—what Mill calls " uniformity of coexistence "—would correspond to the formal cause, at least if any such order could be systematically worked out. Regularity of sequence in the transformations of energy would take the place of the efficient cause. But, if a humanistic point of view is to be accepted, it would be necessary to believe that all these modes of explanation are subordinate in the end to the idea of the good. This would not mean, I take it, that there is some good being, apart from and distinct from all other individuals, who, by his inherent power, produces them—this would be to reintroduce efficiency as ultimate ; but rather that the universe is to be understood as being such that the best is, in the end, that which tends to be evolved in it. The universe is thus interpreted in the light of the conception which seems to make our own human action intelligible.*

* It must surely appear, on reflection, to be a very curious prejudice which leads the ordinary consciousness to suppose that a thing is sufficiently explained if it can be shown to have been pushed, but not if it can only be shown to have been drawn. Yet, even in the physical world, the conception that has thrown most

(4) *On Time.*—Any such view of the universe as
that now suggested is at once met by a very serious
difficulty connected with the idea of time. It is
urged that ultimate reality must be thought of as
eternal, and cannot consequently be represented
as a time-process directed towards an end. This
objection is as old as Parmenides, who turned it
against the idea of process contained in the doctrine
of Heraclitus ; and it appears to have been used by
him and his followers to deny the reality of all motion
and change.   It is essentially the same idea that
is at the bottom of Spinoza's objection to teleology.
The real, he thinks, cannot be supposed to be aiming
at anything beyond itself ; it must be intrinsically
self-sufficient and at rest.   In more modern times,
again, Kant has sought to show that time can only
be regarded as empirically real, and cannot be accepted as a determination of the noumenal world.

light on the general structure of the system in which we live is
the conception of a force of attraction operating, if not at a distance, at any rate through a distance ; and, though some
modern physicists have attempted to explain this away, they
do not appear as yet to have been very successful in their efforts.
The Platonic view, which I am here seeking, in a manner, to re-
vive, is to the effect that the attractiveness of the good may in
the end be at least as satisfactory a principle of explanation as
either physical attraction or transference of motion.   Of course,
I do not mean that the exact form that Plato gave to this
conception can be accepted as adequate ; but, in many ways,
his statement of it still remains more suggestive than that of
any one else.

Now, if we seriously accept the idea of the good as giving us a key to the secret of the universe, we seem to be accepting a time-process as having ultimate reality. Some seek to escape this difficulty by the application of the conception of " degrees of reality " ; and there is no doubt a sense in which this conception is valid and important.* Often, however, it seems to me to be a somewhat confusing notion, and may be used merely to save ourselves the trouble of facing ultimate difficulties. It will not do to take our stand on contradictions, and seek to save ourselves by affirming that the modes of existence in which they are involved have only a certain degree of reality. What, then, are we to say to this fundamental objection ?

I think we must say, in the first place, that this difficulty about time is on the whole the most fundamental and the most obstinate in the whole range of philosophy ; and that it can only be adequately dealt with, if at all, in a complete system of meta-

* The doctrine of " Degrees of Reality " in its most modern form (for it has a long history) is, I think, best expounded in Bradley's *Appearance and Reality* and in Caird's *Evolution of Theology in the Greek Philosophers.* The treatment of it in Mr. A. E. Taylor's *Elements of Metaphysics* is also highly instructive. There are two important points that seem to me to be brought out by these writers. The first is that we ought to recognize degrees of adequacy in our apprehension of reality. This seems

physics—certainly not in a series of somewhat casual lectures such as these. It might be prudent to content myself with this general statement here ; but I cannot think that it would be very satisfactory. Presumptuous as it may seem, therefore, I must try to indicate, however inadequately, what I believe to be the solution of this great problem, or, at least, what is the direction in which the solution must be sought.

The simplest way, and I think a quite true way, of putting it is to say that the order of time must be accepted as real, but that its transience must be

to be on the whole quite correctly expressed by the phrase " Degrees of Truth," though I should prefer to call it " grades " or " stages " in truth. The second is that the objects that we apprehend may, in their own nature, be nearer to or further from the whole, which alone is, in the full sense, real. Thus a stone is further removed from the whole than a man, though both are contained within the whole, and both must be held to be expressions of the nature of the whole. I think it would be somewhat less misleading to use the phrase " Grades of Actuality " to express this distinction, rather than " Degrees of Reality." The whole and all its aspects must, I think, be regarded as real ; but certainly we can hardly suppose, as Spinoza appears sometimes to do, that the expression of the nature of the whole is " as full and perfect in a hair as heart." It is against this view that the conception of " Degrees of Reality " is primarily directed. But what I am anxious to guard against is what seems to me the dangerous misconception that we can solve any problem about a part or aspect of the universe by saying that it has only a certain degree of reality. If we are to deal with it satisfactorily we must seek to show the exact place that it holds in the system of reality, and how such a place is compatible with the conception of that system as a whole.

Q

regarded as illusory. In our ordinary way of thinking, we seem to take our stand upon the present,
which alone has real existence. We suppose that the
past was real when we experienced it, but that it has
ceased to be so ; and that the future has not yet
become real. It seems clear that this cannot be an
ultimately correct way of thinking. If it were,
nothing whatever could be, in any ultimate sense,
real. We should be back again at the Heraclitean
flux. We should have to suppose that at every
moment something is becoming real, and, in the
very act of doing so, is losing its reality.* Now, it
may be noted that, in our ordinary common-sense
view of things, we are not in the habit of thinking
of space in any similar fashion. When we pass from
one place to another, we do not imagine that the
place from which we have gone is any less real than
that with which our experience is now concerned.
We habitually think of space as objective, and as
somehow subsisting whether we experience it or no.

---

* It may be noted, in passing, that this was the view of Descartes. Hence he held that the conservation of anything meant,
in reality, its re-creation from moment to moment. The objection that naturally occurs is—If so, how is the Conservator
himself conserved ? Does his existence also come into being
and drop out again at every moment ? If not, why should we
suppose that the existence of anything else does so ? It is vain
to answer that the Conservator is not in time ; for, if so, how
can he act in time ?

Time we are much more apt to think of as purely subjective, and as existing only at the moment at which we are experiencing it. It is this view, I think, that we ought to learn to transcend. We should invert the step that was taken by Berkeley. He tried to give to space the subjectivity which in our ordinary view is ascribed only to time. We must, on the contrary, endeavour to give to time the objectivity which we are apt only to allow to space.* We must, that is to say, think of reality as permanent, the past and the future existing quite as truly as the present. But this need not lead us to deny the reality of the time-order. The real universe may be a series of events, starting from a definite beginning and leading up to a definite end (or rather, perhaps, forming a closed circle, in which the end and the beginning are identical),† even if we deny that the process dis-

---

* Clifford, as I understand, once put forward the view that time might be regarded as the " fourth dimension " of space, for which some mathematicians have been in search. From a philosophical point of view, this is certainly not as absurd as it is apt at first to appear. At any rate, if we negate the transitoriness of time, it is much less far removed from space than it is on the more common view. It seems clear also that, if we could imagine a being living simply in a one-dimensional space, that space would have for him a purely temporal character.

† The last member in the time series can hardly be thought of as followed by nothing, or by an empty time. It seems necessary therefore, to think of it as being immediately followed by the

appears when the end is reached. In this sense
it may be possible to reconcile the idea of eternity
with that of time, and to recognize, with Parmenides,
that the universe is permanent, while yet we hold
also, with Heraclitus, that it contains a process. I
cannot here enlarge further upon this conciliation ;
but I believe it will be found that it contains the
essential elements for the solution of this most
bewildering of all problems.* At any rate, it may
help us to see that the attempt to solve this problem
is not (as it is often apt to be thought) an altogether
hopeless one ; and that we need not allow it per-
manently to block the way to any intelligible
interpretation of the universe.

(5) *On Ultimate Reality.*—After these explanations,
it may now be possible to sum up what we are to
understand by a humanistic conception of ultimate
reality. It amounts essentially to trying to think

first member ; and we are thus led inevitably to the conception
(an old enough one in philosophical speculation) of recurring
cycles. This seems to be a necessary part of the general conception of the finite infinite, which appears to be the only intelligible conception of infinity. On this point I may refer to a
paper on "The Infinite and the Perfect" in *Mind.* Aristotle, it
may be noted, held a view very closely approximating to this
(see especially the twelfth book of his *Metaphysics*, and cf.
Caird's *Evolution of Theology in the Greek Philosophers*, Lecture
XIV).

   * If the view here indicated is anything like the truth, time
would be not merely—what Plato called it—" the moving image
of eternity," but rather, in a sense, eternity itself.

of the universe as an ethical unity, in which the most excellent forms of life are developed through a continuous process. To us, as occupying a certain stage in this eternal movement, it necessarily presents itself in a somewhat inadequate and misleading aspect. We pass from point to point in the unfolding of our lives ; and what is behind and before us seems almost to sink into the abyss of nothingness. Our present puzzles and difficulties also press upon us with a weight altogether out of proportion to their intrinsic significance. In the light of eternity they would appear to be of hardly any consequence. Yet they are not unreal. They are aspects in the ever-growing life of the one great reality in which all things are.

This reality has to be thought of as a many in one. It has as its basis the material system, spreading out around us, not indeed to infinity, but to an incalculable extent, yet bound together by unity of system and persistence of motion throughout the whole of its incessant changes. Within this material system various qualitative differences emerge. There grows up, in particular, by gradual development, the vast series of living forms, with man at their head, in whom first the universe comes to the consciousness of itself ; and it is in the more and more perfect working out of this life, so far as we can see, that the ultimate meaning of the universe is displayed. What the end of this development would be, it is hardly possible for us, here and now, so much as to imagine. It would seem to mean the perfect unfolding of the intellectual, moral, and æsthetic nature—the realization of that absolute spiritual perfection for which perhaps the name of God, if it is to be used at all,* is most fittingly reserved. The realization of such a being cannot, however, it would seem, be thought of merely as a " far-off divine event," that is to be accomplished once for all, and in the achievement of which everything else may be expected to disappear. Rather in that final accomplishment the whole life of the universe would be preserved and consummated. That perfect intelligence, or those

---

* I admit, of course, that there is a good deal to be said—and a good deal has been said—for avoiding the term " God " altogether in metaphysical discussions. Its meaning in metaphysics is apt to diverge rather too widely from that which it has in religion. But the ethical conception of a completed humanity seems to me at least a good deal nearer to what is involved in the religious consciousness than the somewhat geometrical God of the Cartesians, or even than what may be called the logical God of some more recent writers. Some distinguish the philosophical conception of the Absolute from the religious conception of God. But the latter seems to be at least in the end identical with one aspect of the former—at any rate, if any such view as I have been trying to indicate can be accepted as correct. It should be added that the philosophical term " Absolute " is itself somewhat unsatisfactory, so far as it suggests what is unconditioned.

perfect intelligences,* would turn back upon the universe through which he or they have grown, viewing with perfect insight and approval, and, we may suppose, with ineffable blessedness, the harmonious completeness of that immeasurable system of all things, rolling on through its everlasting cycles.

This is a very brief indication of what I conceive to be the nature of ultimate reality. Perhaps the statement is too summary to be readily intelligible. Happily, there are several recent writers who have worked out the conception of its nature with considerable fullness—notably F. H. Bradley, Josiah Royce, J. E. McTaggart, and A. E. Taylor.† I must confess, however, that the views of these writers are not entirely in harmony with one another, and that it is by no means certain that the view that I have here briefly indicated is quite in harmony with any of them; and I cannot here discuss the nature or grounds of these divergences. Perhaps, on the whole, the view of A. E. Taylor is most nearly in harmony with that

* Whether the completed Intelligence is to be thought of as one or many, seems to me to be a subordinate question, with which, in such a summary as this, we need not concern ourselves.

† The chief works in which the views of these writers are developed are *Appearance and Reality, The World and the Individual, Studies in Hegelian Cosmology* (supplemented by *Some Dogmas of Religion*), and *Elements of Metaphysics.*

indicated above ; but his doctrine of infinity (and consequently of eternity) appears to be somewhat different from that to which I adhere. His view of reality is also, if I understand it rightly, more subjective than the one that I have here sought to indicate. It should be added that Mr. Taylor's view is very largely derived from that of Professor Royce, from which perhaps it does not materially differ. Royce's theory of the infinite (largely derived from Dedekind) is certainly one of the most important contributions to philosophical thought that have been made in recent years, whatever view we may take of its ultimate validity.* Mr. Bradley's view of the absolute, on the other hand, does not appear to me to leave any real place for process. Dr. McTaggart's view is not, I think, very widely different from that of Royce and Taylor ; but it does not seem to me to contain an equally clear and definite conception of the infinite ; and it leans perhaps too decidedly towards pluralism. The writings of the Master of Balliol (especially those dealing with religion) contain, I think, a more satisfactory view of the Absolute than any of those to whom I have here referred ; but their historical setting makes it rather more difficult to

* I am bound to confess that it does not, in the end, seem to me to be valid ; but the objections to which it is open cannot be here considered.

disentangle the final outcome ; and it is possibly true that historical forms of statement are retained in them to a somewhat greater extent than is quite desirable. I have thought it well to give this brief indication of the relation of the point of view which I adopt to that taken by other recent writers ; though it is obviously impossible, in such a sketch as this, to enter into any real discussion of the subject.

(6) *On Good and Evil.*—In connection, however, with such an interpretation of the universe, there is a further difficulty that presents itself to many people as being quite as insuperable as that with regard to the reality of time. This is the difficulty with regard to the reality of the distinction between good and evil. And, indeed, it seems clear that, if the difficulty about time were insuperable, that about good and evil would be so also. The difficulty is briefly this. Such a view as that which has now been set before us may be described as absolutely optimistic. It involves the ultimate triumph of the best. The world has to be thought of, in Leibniz's phrase, as "the best of all possible worlds"; and this must, indeed, be taken to mean (what it did not mean for Leibniz), not merely the best that is actually possible, but the best that is in any real sense conceivable. If so, the question at once

suggests itself, How is it that there is anything that can even be contrasted with the best? Whence comes the element of negativity? No one, as it has been said,* who has ever felt tooth-ache, or who has been conscious of an ungenerous thought, can doubt that there are some things that present themselves to us as painful, ugly, and detestable. If the universe is guided by the idea of the good, why are not these excluded? Why is our experience not all bright and beautiful?

This difficulty seems to me to be quite insuperable for any philosophy, like that of Parmenides or Spinoza, which does not recognize the necessity of the element of negativity†—in other words, for

* See Dr. McTaggart's *Some Dogmas of Religion*, p. 208, where, however, this point is brought forward, perhaps rightly, against the conception of an omnipotent creative God, conceived as existing apart from and prior to the world. The ethical God, as here conceived, is, of course, to be regarded as non-creative, at least in this sense, but rather as self-revealed through an eternal process ; and the conception of omnipotence has hardly any meaning as applied to such a being. It only means that there is nothing that can prevent the realization of the best. It may be well to add here, however, that when Dr. McTaggart speaks of an omnipotent being, he seems to mean one who is entirely unconditioned—surely a meaningless conception.

† The element of negativity has been admirably discussed by Professor Bosanquet in an article published in *Mind* (N.S., vol. xiii.). I may remark that some of the ultimate difficulties in Dr. McTaggart's conception of the Absolute appear to be traceable to the attempt (already noticeable in his *Studies in Hegelian Dialectic*) to eliminate the element of negativity.

any philosophy which does not regard the universe as a process. ⌐It is also insuperable for any philosophy which separates God from the world, as the perfect being from a finite existence which He creates. If He is perfect in Himself, why does He not create a perfect world ? But if we recognize that it is the essential nature of reality to be a developing process, the whole difficulty seems to disappear at once. A process necessarily contains the distinction between the lower and the higher, the beginning and the end. The higher, relatively to the lower, is good ; the lower, relatively to the higher, is evil. ⌐ It might, of course, still be be asked—Why does not the process go continuously upward from the lower to the higher, so that good should never seem to be overcome by evil ? Indeed, it might be urged that it is only such a sinking back from the better that is properly to be described as evil at all. But I think this question is seen to be an almost meaningless one, as soon as we realize to ourselves with any clearness what is meant by the attainment of the good. ⌐The good at which we aim may be most briefly described as the realization of a complete intelligence, which understands and appreciates the universe. There is a process towards the development of this ; but, from the nature of the case, it is a process that must return upon itself, and include that from which it starts. It is not the mere antithesis of that from which it sets out, but the necessary complement which gives it meaning. The higher, in short, would not be higher if it did not, in the end, include the lower in itself.

On the whole, I think we may say that we have no real ground for supposing that it is possible, in any real sense, to conceive a better universe than that which we are gradually getting to know.* What is apt at times to lead us to think so, is the false emphasis that we tend to lay upon the present. The pains and difficulties of the present moment are often so absorbing and overwhelming that we cannot put them into their proper relations to the past and future, which indeed even seem to us to be non-existent. There is no real ground for thinking that if we saw the universe in its totality any of the events in it would seem to be out of place. Even toothache may be necessary for the development of fortitude and sympathy.

* When Dr. Rashdall, for instance, affirms that " a better universe is imaginable " (*Theory of Good and Evil*, vol. ii. p. 341), one would like to know whether the better universe that he imagines includes those human excellences which we only know of through their development and exercise in relation to the difficulties, dangers, and imperfections of the world in which we are. If not, how can he be sure that the universe that he imagines is really a better one ?

Even ungenerous thoughts may be the means by which we learn our limitations, and grow to a more complete perfection. In short, the whole difficulty vanishes when we think—or, at least, *would* vanish if we were able consistently to think—of the universe as a complex process, in which the highest and most comprehensive modes of spiritual life are being gradually realized through conflict.

It would carry me far beyond the limits of this discussion if I were to attempt, even in the most meagre outline, to consider how far such a view of life as is here indicated involves the persistence of the individual consciousness throughout a time-process. It may be urged that, in order to work it out with any completeness, it might be necessary for us (like Dr. McTaggart and some other recent writers) to make use of the conception of reincarnation, and perhaps even of something at least akin to what the Buddhists express by such terms as " karma." But there may also be other ways in which the difficulties can be met. At any rate, this is a vast and complicated subject, upon which it does not seem necessary to enter here. To discuss it would involve, among other things, the consideration of what is to be understood by personal identity, and by the unity of an individual life. But we may at least say that the fact that the process of development towards that completed insight which would grasp the whole, is one that seems to us long, painful, intricate, and even at times unavailing, does not appear to present any real dfficulty. The universe has plenty of time, and may well be able to make good its apparent failures, and include them in a larger harmony, whatever its methods of doing so may be. This is enough for our present purpose. I am not trying here to solve the enigmas of the universe, but only urging that we need not regard them as insoluble.

(7) *On the Nature of Proof.*—But, it may still be asked, Allowing that there is no ground for the rejection of such a view of the universe, is there any positive ground for affirming it ? Is it not of the nature of those metaphysical speculations which Kant compared with the visions of the theosophist, as being almost as fantastic and quite as incapable of proof ? Now, there is a sense in which I think it may be admitted—indeed, a sense in which it ought to be strenuously maintained—that a metaphysical theory must, from the nature of the case, be incapable of any proof. Probably no worse service was ever rendered to philosophy than that contained in the Cartesian effort to establish speculative principles after the manner of geometry.*

* To say this is, I hope, not incompatible with the recognition that the Cartesians did more than any other school of writers for

It introduced an altogether false and fatal conception of the kind of proof of which such principles are capable—a conception from which more recent writers have found it very difficult to emancipate their minds. It seems clear, however, that the fundamental nature of things cannot be deduced from anything more fundamental than itself. In the end, the only proof that can be given of a metaphysical theory is the fact that it makes the universe, as we know it, intelligible to us, and that we cannot think of any other theory that does. Hence, as both Plato and Hegel saw, if there is to be a systematic proof of an ultimate metaphysical doctrine, the proof must be, not mathematical, but dialectical in its character. That is to say, we can only establish it by showing the insufficiency of all possible alternatives. It may be doubtful, of course, whether either Plato or Hegel succeeded in doing this. It might even be urged that they can hardly both have succeeded ; for it seems clear that their views are not quite identical. It may be, however, that the one pro-

the development of modern philosophy, as well as that of the mathematical and physical sciences ; and that some of them— especially Spinoza—showed, in spite of a mistaken method, a degree of insight into the bearings of philosophical problems that has hardly ever been surpassed. What Goethe says of the good man is true of the good philosopher, that, in all his wanderings, he retains some consciousness of the right way.

vided the suggestion for what has been more
adequately carried out by the other. They have
at least this in common, that they both take their
stand on the highest and most comprehensive of
all the facts that are presented to us within the
universe of our experience, viz. the spiritual
life of man. They both succeed, moreover, in
making it at least reasonably clear that it is
not really possible to explain this great fact by
means of any of the lower and less comprehensive
facts around it. If so, it would seem that it must
be explained from within, or from something still
higher than itself, or from something entirely beyond
the reach of our experience ; or that it must be
incapable of any explanation at all. The only
alternatives that are left to us, therefore, are some
form of humanism, some kind of supernatural
revelation, agnosticism, and pure scepticism. The
last would, of course, only be the refuge of despair.
The second and third, however, are hardly distinguishable from it, at least from the point of view
of intelligible explanation, except in so far as
they present us with some positive principle by
which our life in this universe can be accounted
for. Now, it is hard to see how such a principle—
a principle capable of throwing light upon our
experience—can be anything altogether beyond

the reach of our experience ; and, as a matter of fact, we constantly find that both agnostics and the adherents of the various forms of revealed religion do state their ultimate explanations, when they try to give them any positive form, in modes that are essentially humanistic. On the whole, therefore, we seem to be led to the conclusion that some form of humanism is the only possible method of making our universe intelligible to ourselves. That it can be somehow made intelligible, is a conviction from which it is hardly possible for us to escape, in view of the continuous progress that has been made in our knowledge of the world around us, and of the development of our own conscious experience. It is hardly possible for us really to doubt that our universe must somehow be an intelligible system. At the same time, it is obvious enough that the attempt to understand the whole must be surrounded with difficulties of a very different order from those that are encountered when we are only trying to understand some particular part in relation to others. We can hardly hope that a philosophical system will be completed as a rounded whole, in the sense in which a system of geometry or geology may conceivably be completed. It must probably always be of a somewhat more tentative character, and liable to more constant changes through the

R

growth of our general experience of the world.*
But this need not, I think, drive us to scepticism
or agnosticism, or to any dark revelations that are
hardly distinguishable from these. We need not
despair of seeing a philosophical system sufficiently
completed to become a guide, a power, and an inspiration in our lives. If we are right in believing
that life is essentially a process, it is certainly not
surprising that we cannot attain to everything at
once. We might even say, with Mr. Balfour, " What
would be a world which we could understand ? "
And we might add (if, indeed, it is anything different), What would be a world which we could at
once apprehend as being complete and perfect ?
But to any such questions I think we should add
also some such comment as that of the late Professor Wallace.† Admitting that a world "which
we had thoroughly understood" (and which we were
not, for that very reason, recreating for ourselves

---

* I should even be prepared to concede to the agnostic that,
from the point of view of a completed consciousness, any account
of the Absolute that has ever been given, even by the best of
metaphysicians, from Plato and Aristotle to Spinoza, Hegel,
Bradley, and Royce, would appear to be almost ridiculously wide
of the mark. But this fact (if such it be) does not destroy, nor
does it even seriously diminish, the relative truth and value of
such attempts. Glimpses of the truth are not the same as
perfect insight ; but they are also not the same as absolute
ignorance.

† *Lectures and Essays on Natural Theology and Ethics,* p. 97.

by sharing in the process of its growth) would be for us " a world, clearly, without interest ; the den of listlessness and dumb despair ; or rather the ice-age of humanity, when to be and not to be would for once be absolutely alike " ; we may yet go on to ask further, " But, on the other hand, what were a world which we did *not* understand, had not in any measure understood ?   A world full of fears rather than hopes ; a perpetual uncertainty, a grisly mystery. . . . The world which reason claims is one where she may go for ever on and never die ; a world where nothing can be called utterly unknowable, though much may remain for ever unknown ; a world where, as humanity accumulates more and more its intellectual and spiritual capital, we shall move about more and more freely, i.e. more and more wisely."   This seems to me to express very well the ultimate attitude of a sound philosophy ; and it is an attitude which, in a certain large sense, admitting all the qualifications that have been urged, may still quite fairly be described as humanistic.

PLYMOUTH
WILLIAM BRENDON AND SON, LTD.
PRINTERS